JOINED AT THE HEART

Quilting for Family and Friends

ANNE MOSCICKI
AND LINDA WYCKOFF-HICKEY

Martingale®
& COMPANY

Credits

President ◆ Nancy J. Martin

CEO ◆ Daniel J. Martin

VP and General Manager ◆ Tom Wierzbicki

Publisher ◆ Jane Hamada

Editorial Director ◆ Mary V. Green

Managing Editor ◆ Tina Cook

Technical Editor ◆ Darra Williamson

Copy Editor ◆ Melissa Bryan

Design Director ◆ Stan Green

Illustrators ◆ Robin Strobel and Laurel Strand

Cover and Text Designer ◆ Regina Girard

Photographer ◆ Brent Kane

That Patchwork Place® is an imprint of Martingale & Company®.

Joined at the Heart:
Quilting for Family and Friends

© 2005 by Anne Moscicki and Linda Wyckoff-Hickey

Martingale & Company
20205 144th Avenue NE
Woodinville, WA 98072-8478 USA
www.martingale-pub.com

Printed in China
10 09 08 07 06 05   8 7 6 5 4 3 2 1

Library of Congress Cataloging-in-Publication Data

Moscicki, Anne.
  Joined at the heart: quilting for family and friends / Anne Moscicki and Linda Wyckoff-Hickey.
    p. cm.
  ISBN 1-56477-604-2
1. Patchwork—Patterns. 2. Quilting. 3. Patchwork quilts. I. Wyckoff-Hickey, Linda. II. Title.
  TT835.M6896 2005
  746.46—dc22
                                              2005003494

Mission Statement

Dedicated to providing quality products and service to inspire creativity.

Acknowledgments

As the projects in this book took shape, we have been grateful for:

The patient support of our husbands, John Moscicki and Patrick Hickey, who have given us the opportunity to stretch our talents in new directions;

The talented staff at Martingale & Company, including Karen Soltys, Mary Green, and Tina Cook, for their guidance; Darra Williamson for her cheer and enthusiastic technical editing; Melissa Bryan for rounding out the text; and Stan Green, Brent Kane, and Regina Girard for their creative contributions;

Deb Hollister for her hospitality and steady insight;

Cindy Pope for inspiring the Scotch Granny in all of us;

The talents of both our annual retreat pals and the Calendar Girls for contributing to the group projects;

The generous staffs at Ravenna Gardens and Frederick E. Squire III Antiques in lovely downtown Lake Oswego for loaning us some beautiful props for photography;

Celeste Marshall, Amy Helmkamp, and Linda Humfeld for the beautiful quilting that has pulled all our designs together into real quilts;

The encouragement of our families and friends, including Mimi and Jack Teters, Yvonne Moscicki, and Richard Wyckoff;

And finally, each and every one of our exuberant, creative, adventurous, and independent children, for their inspiration, interruptions, and constant reminders of what life is all about.

CONTENTS

Star Pillows

Be Brave

Checkerboard

Scotch Granny

Hummingbirds

QUILTING CONNECTIONS

Just what is it about a quilt, the quality each one possesses that stops us in our tracks for a closer look?

Whether humble patchwork or elaborately stitched heirloom, each quilt has a story to tell of its maker and her sense of purpose and pride. Fabrics speak of extravagance or frugality, colors whisper or shout the maker's joy, a unique embellishment might tell us of her imagination, signed blocks of her friends or community. And while tiny stitches may speak to us of patience, large ones might tell us she preferred the great outdoors!

Each quilt possesses a generosity of spirit bequeathed upon it by its maker—and generous makers we are!

We begin with a search for designs to serve as a warm embrace across thousands of miles, or just across the room. We seek out cheery prints and jazzy colors that promise brighter days, or soft shades and warm textures to take the place of a hug. And then, we start stitching . . .

Quilts mark graduations, marriages, first homes, and golden anniversaries. We make quilts for the babies whose parents we love, and quilts that we hope will wrap our children and grandchildren in love's warmth long after we are able.

We make quilts to honor those stricken by disease, and to fund the fight against their afflictions. We quilt to thank the exceptional teachers, soldiers, officers, doctors, and nurses who insist that they were only doing their job.

And we're still not done stitching. We make quilts for children we'll never even meet, sending them into our communities to heal the pain of abuse and loss. We pack them up and ship them halfway around the world to form bonds beyond language, destined for survivors and orphans. We piece together quilts that seek to change the world by quieting a distant cry, extending a helping hand, or offering a measure of hope.

So, how does a collection of scraps become an object that speaks to the heart? Each and every quilt has one amazing thing in common: it is infused with the powerful thoughtfulness of the maker.

SHARING STITCHES

Linda feels the miles evaporate when her best friend, halfway across the country, has a rough day and calls to cry, wrapped in one of the identical tulip quilts Linda made to honor their longstanding bond of friendship.

Anne's mom shares the blossoms of the magnificent cherry tree blooming in her front yard with her faraway sister by stitching a basketful of blushing pink prints into a classic pattern, so they both can enjoy its fleeting, frothy pink boughs.

Going through a basket of scraps for a new project, Anne comes across fabric left over from the quilt that brought members of her family together to tell part of the story of her grandfather's life.

Elaborate or simple, quilts like these connect us within our world, and join us at the heart. We feel the appreciation of friends and family, and take satisfaction in seeing our quilted expressions on display or lovingly used.

And then we take an extra step, casting the work of our hands far wider than our circle of family and friends, farther than we can see, even though it's too simple to believe that a quilt could mend every problem in the world. Could the beauty of an embroidered flower allow a young mother in a war-ravaged country even a moment to think herself worthy of the threads and thoughts of someone on the other side of the planet? Could the playful safari print on a simple turned-edge quilt allow a bruised child to imagine himself the master of dangerous adventures as he drifts off to sleep?

That's the chance we all seem willing to take in the thousands upon thousands of quilts given to a multitude of strangers every year. Whether they are accompanied by the blessing of a congregation or a single quilter's desire to fill the need for warmth, our aching hope is that they will change someone's life for the better. At the very least, we enrich ourselves by exercising our compassion, as we imagine another's distress.

JOY IN THE MAKING

The joy is not merely the delight of the recipient, but the process of creating. The time we spend quilting is a personal journey, and we revel in new ideas as we put our own twist on the traditional, pairing colors and prints with either abandon or precision. Each time we take up needle and thread, we put our day in order, piecing chaos into beautiful patterns as we stitch connections, one scrap at a time.

Quilting with others adds the delights of collaboration, a connection to community. Many of us have treasured memories of bonds formed as we learned to quilt from a grandmother, mother, or friend. In turn, sharing our skills with others multiplies the joy.

FROM THE HEART

All of the quilts and projects collected here are about sharing your skills, memories, hopes, time, and love. We truly enjoyed making each one, and we hope you'll be as excited about creating them for the people who matter to you. We've included variations for Make It Unique!, Make It Simple!, and Make It with Friends!, and we invite you to use our techniques and suggestions to make each project as one-of-a-kind as its intended recipient—even if that's you! Our sincerest wish is that you feel inspired to savor the time you spend quilting.

Happy stitching!

Anne & Linda

FIRESIDE SNUGGLER QUILT

As a teenager, I spent winter afternoons on ice skates, swooping, twirling, and gliding with my best friend. Afterward we'd tromp back through the snow to her house, where we were welcomed by her grandmother, Dearie. Hot tea, cookies, and conversation warmed us from the inside out, as we wrapped up in blankets and quilts by the roaring old brick fireplace. The stories, laughter, and sense of belonging that Dearie fostered in the firelight warm me still.
—Linda

MATERIALS

Yardage is based on 42"-wide fabric unless otherwise noted. We used decorator-weight fabric for the quilt top and snuggly flannel for the backing and binding.

1¾ yards of tone-on-tone print or solid for first, third, fifth, and outside borders and cornerstones

1⅝ yards of theme fabric for center panel and fourth border

⅜ yard *each* of 5 coordinating prints for pieced (piano key) borders

3⅞ yards of fabric for backing

⅝ yard of fabric for binding

66" x 66" piece of batting

CUTTING

Cut all strips from the crosswise grain unless otherwise noted.

From *each* of the 5 coordinating prints, cut:

◆ 5 strips, 2" x 40" (25 total). You will have one strip left over.

From the tone-on-tone print or solid, cut:

◆ 10 strips, 2" x 40"

◆ 7 strips, 4½" x 40"; subcut 1 strip into 8 squares, 4½" x 4½"

From the *lengthwise grain* of the theme fabric, cut:

◆ 2 strips, 4¾" x 41"

From the remaining theme fabric, cut:

◆ 2 strips, 4¾" x 32½"

◆ 1 square, 18½" x 18½"

From the binding fabric, cut:

◆ 6 strips, 2½" x 40"

ASSEMBLING THE PIECED (PIANO KEY) BORDERS

1. Sew one 2"-wide strip of each coordinating print together along the long edges to make a strip set as shown; press. Make four strip sets, varying the fabric placement in each one. Cut each strip set into seven segments, 4½" wide (28 total).

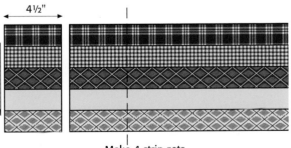

Make 4 strip sets.
Cut 28 segments.

Fireside Snuggler Quilt

By Anne Moscicki and Linda Wyckoff-Hickey,
60" x 60". Quilted by Celeste Marshall.

2. Sew four of the remaining 2"-wide coordinating print strips together along the long edges to make a strip set as shown; press. Cut the strip set into eight segments, 4½" wide.

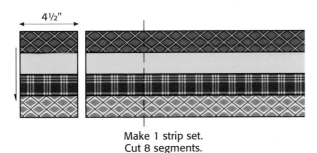

Make 1 strip set.
Cut 8 segments.

3. Join two segments from step 1 and one segment from step 2 side by side to make a pieced border unit as shown; press. Make four. Sew a 4½" tone-on-tone square to each end of a pieced border unit; press. Make two. Label these four units pieced border 1.

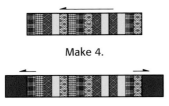

Make 4.

Sew squares to 2 of the 4.

4. Join five segments from step 1 and one segment from step 2 side by side to make a pieced border unit as shown; press. Make four. Sew a 4½" tone-on-tone square to each end of a pieced border unit; press. Make two. Label these four units pieced border 2.

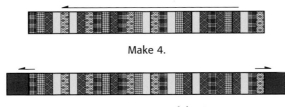

Make 4.

Sew squares to 2 of the 4.

ASSEMBLING THE QUILT TOP

Refer to "Adding a Straight Border" on page 106 as needed to measure, join and/or trim, and sew on the border strips.

1. Use two 2"-wide tone-on-tone or solid strips to add the first border to the sides, top, and bottom of the 18½" square center panel as shown; press.

2. Add pieced border 1 from step 3 as shown; press.

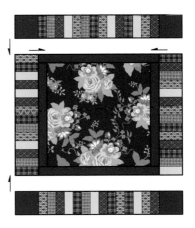

3. Use four 2"-wide tone-on-tone or solid strips to add the third border to the sides, top, and bottom of the quilt as shown; press.

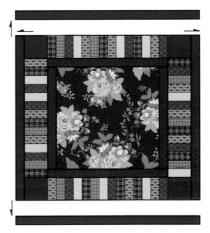

4. Add 4¾" x 32½" theme fabric strips to the sides and 4¾" x 41" theme fabric strips to the top and bottom of the quilt to make the fourth border as shown; press.

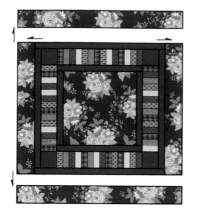

5. Use four 2"-wide tone-on-tone or solid strips to add the fifth border to the sides, top, and bottom of the quilt as shown; press.

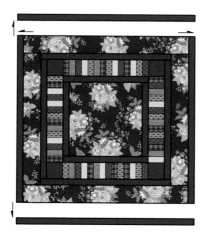

6. Add pieced border 2 from step 4 as shown; press.

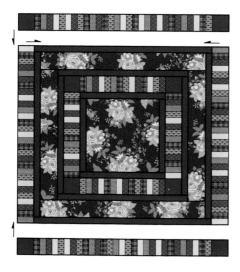

7. Use the 4½"-wide tone-on-tone or solid strips to add the outside border to the sides, top, and bottom of the quilt as shown; press.

FINISHING THE QUILT

1. Refer to "Quilting Basics" on page 104 as needed to finish your quilt. Prepare the quilt backing, and then layer and baste together the backing, batting, and quilt top.

2. Quilt as desired. In the pictured quilt, a symmetrical arrangement of ribbons and leaves begins in the center and expands into rows of swirls and floral garlands that radiate to the quilt edges.

3. Trim the excess batting and backing fabric, remove the basting, and use the 2½"-wide strips to bind your quilt.

4. Add a hanging sleeve, label, or pocket to your quilt, if desired. Refer to "Finishing Touches" on page 109 for methods, tips, and ideas.

QUILTED KINDLING CARRIER

By Anne Moscicki and Linda Wyckoff-Hickey, 17½" x 30½".

MATERIALS

Yardage is based on 42"-wide fabric unless otherwise noted.

⅝ yard of theme fabric for center panel

⅜ yard of tone-on-tone print or solid for frame

⅛ yard *each* of 5 coordinating prints for pieced (piano key) ends

22" x 36" piece of muslin or scrap fabric for lining

18" x 31" piece of oilcloth or imitation suede or leather for backing

22" x 36" piece of batting

3 yards of wide grosgrain ribbon or cotton webbing for handles

Sewing-machine needle suitable for leather

CUTTING

Cut all strips from the crosswise grain.

From the tone-on-tone print or solid, cut:
- 4 strips, 2" x 42"; subcut:
    - 1 strip into 2 strips, 2" x 15½"
    - 2 strips into 1 strip each, 2" x 29½" (2 total)
    - 1 strip into 2 strips, 2" x 18½"

From the theme fabric, cut:
- 1 piece, 15½" x 18½"

From *each* of the 5 coordinating prints, cut:
- 1 strip, 2" x 42" (5 total)

PIECING THE CARRIER

1. Sew a 2" x 15½" tone-on-tone or solid strip to each short edge of the center panel as shown; press.

2. Sew the five 2"-wide coordinating print strips together along the long edges to make a strip set. Press the seams open. Cut the strip set into four segments, 4½" wide. Arrange the segments side by side in pairs as shown and stitch to make two 4½" x 15½" pieced units; press.

4½"

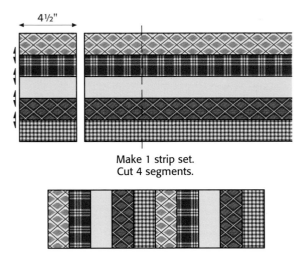

Make 1 strip set.
Cut 4 segments.

Make 2.

3. Sew one unit from step 2 to each end of the unit from step 1 as shown; press.

4. Sew a 2" x 29½" tone-on-tone or solid strip to each side of the unit from step 3 as shown; press.

5. Sew a 2" x 18½" tone-on-tone or solid strip to the top and bottom of the unit from step 4 as shown; press.

QUILTING

Layer the pieced top with the batting and the muslin or scrap fabric for lining, referring to "Quilting Basics" on page 104 as necessary. Quilt the top. We quilted a diamond pattern over the center panel and the pieced (piano key) borders, and we added concentric lines in the frames by following the edge of the sewing machine's ¼" foot. Trim the excess lining and batting even with the edges of the carrier top.

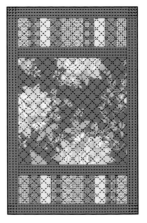

ASSEMBLING THE CARRIER

1. Layer the backing over the quilted layers, right sides together, aligning the fabric edges.

2. Secure a few pins on each of the four sides to hold the layers in place. Double-pin in two places on one long side, placing the pins 10" apart.

3. Stitch the layers ¼" from the edges, beginning at one double-pinned spot and ending at the other to leave a 10" opening as shown.

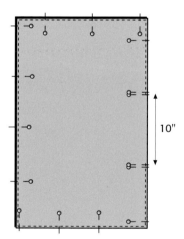

10"

4. Clip the corners at a 45° angle. Turn the carrier right side out through the 10" opening. Use a tool with a blunt tip, such as a chopstick, to square the corners.

5. Pin the opening closed, tucking in the raw edges. Whipstitch the opening closed.

6. Stitch around all four sides a scant ¼" from the edge.

ADDING THE HANDLES

1. Fold one end of the ribbon or webbing under 1"; press.

2. Pin the ribbon or webbing parallel to, and 3" from, the finished long edges of the front of the carrier as shown. Allow 20" for each handle. When you've finished pinning the handle, trim the end and tuck it under the 1" fold.

3. Topstitch the handle down on each side, securing with a stitched square at the eight points where the ribbon crosses the frame. Gather some firewood and settle in for your cozy evening by the hearth!

3¾"

Beanbag Massager

By Anne Moscicki and Linda Wyckoff-Hickey, approximately 6" x 5" x 2".

Tough day at the sewing machine? These lumpy little beanbags may not seem exciting at first glance, but never before have a fat quarter, a little stitching, and a bag of dried beans worked so beautifully to soothe the kinks from a tough day! Now you just need someone to trade backrubs with…

Materials for One Beanbag

1 fat quarter of fabric

1 pound of dried beans, such as chickpeas or garbanzos

1 decorative button (optional)

ASSEMBLING THE BEANBAG

1. Cut one 14" square from the fat quarter. On the wrong side, mark the square diagonally from corner to corner in both directions. Cut the marked square in half once diagonally as shown.

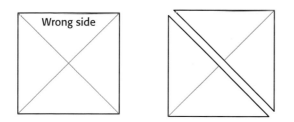

2. Trace the oval pattern on page 18 onto paper or template material. Be sure to include the alignment points on the two long sides. Cut out along the traced line.

3. Layer the triangles right sides together with the raw edges aligned. Position the template on top of the triangle layers, aligning the template edges at the fabric edge and the alignment points on the template with the marked line on the triangle. Mark the edge of the oval on the corner of the triangle. Trim the corner point on the marked curve to create a rounded edge.

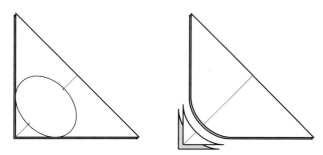

4. Sew around the edge of the layered triangles with a ¼" seam as shown, leaving an approximate 3" opening along the top edge. Make a second row of stitches along the curved edge of the triangle shape to reinforce the seam.

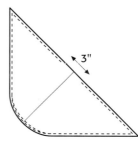

5. Turn the unit right side out and flatten, aligning the seams. Measure and mark 5½" from the end points toward the center of the massager, and add a double row of stitching to the triangle points on each end to create the "handles" as shown.

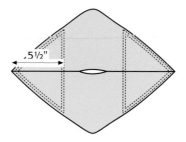

6. Fill the bag with beans and whipstitch the opening closed. Flip the bottom handle up and tack its point to the base of the top handle with a few hand stitches as shown.

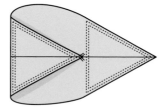

7. Flip the top handle down over the massager. Secure it with a few hand stitches if desired. You may add a decorative button to one end if you'd like to embellish your Beanbag Massager.

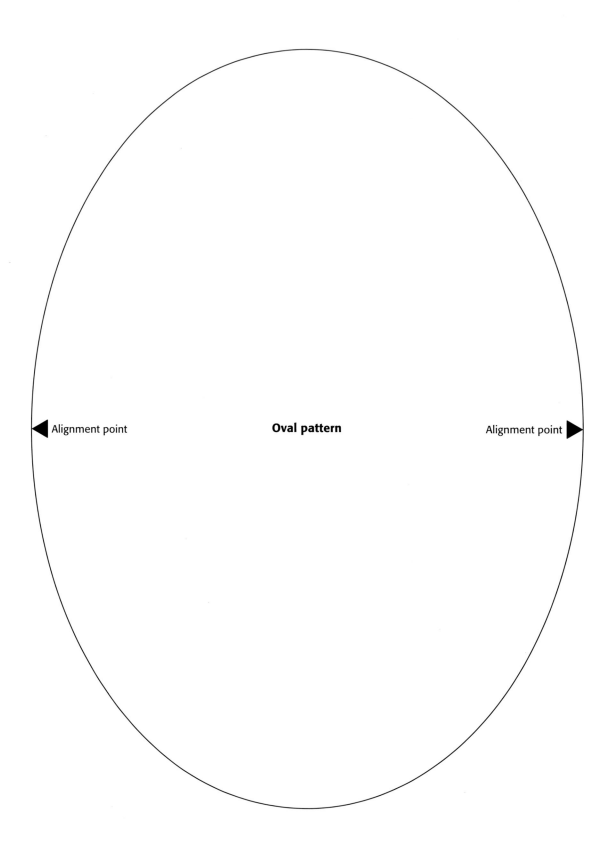

Alignment point ◀   **Oval pattern**   Alignment point ▶

PATHWAYS QUILT

Warm sunshine sparkles on a chilly Idaho creek, and I listen to the shrieks and cheers of my daughters and their cousins wading out to the big rock in the middle. It's the same rock that the kids of my generation waded out to in the same noisy way, years ago! Watching the members of this new generation find their way fills me with the most satisfying of memories. Our family cabin is just up the hill from this spot, and bringing my children back along these paths links my past and my future.

—Anne

MATERIALS

Yardage is based on 42"-wide fabric unless otherwise noted.

1¼ yards of fabric for outer border

1⅛ yards (total) of light prints for bars

⅝ yard of fabric for inner border

¼ yard *each* of 16 coordinating prints for blocks

1 fat quarter of fabric for bar accents

4½ yards of fabric for backing

¾ yard of fabric for binding

74" x 80" piece of batting

CUTTING

Cut all strips from the crosswise grain.

From the fat quarter, cut:

◆ 3 strips, 2½" x 20"; subcut each strip into 8 squares, 2½" x 2½" (24 total). You will have 2 squares left over.

From the light prints, cut a *total* of:

◆ 7 strips, 5" x 40"; subcut each strip into 15 rectangles, 2½" x 5" (105 total). You will have 9 rectangles left over.

From *each* of the 16 coordinating prints, cut:

◆ 3 strips, 2" x 40" (48 total)

From the inner-border fabric, cut:

◆ 6 strips, 2½" x 40"

From the outer-border fabric, cut:

◆ 7 strips, 5½" x 40"

From the binding fabric, cut:

◆ 8 strips, 2½" x 40"

Pathways Quilt

By Anne Moscicki and Linda Wyckoff-Hickey,
68" x 74". Quilted by Celeste Marshall.

MAKING THE BAR ACCENT UNITS

Place one 2½" bar accent square over one end of a 2½" x 5" light rectangle, right sides together and aligning the raw edges. Mark the square once diagonally from corner to corner. Sew on the marked line. Trim the seam, leaving a ¼" seam allowance. Fold the corner out; press. Make 22 bar accent units, 11 of each variation.

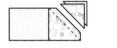

Make 11.

Make 11.

ASSEMBLING THE PATHWAYS BLOCKS

1. Sew three assorted 2"-wide strips together along the long edges to make a strip set; press the seam allowances open. Make 16 strip sets, varying the fabric combinations as much as possible. Cut each strip set into six segments, 6½" wide (96 total).

6½"

Make 16 strip sets.
Cut 96 segments.

2. Stitch a bar accent unit to a segment from step 1; press. Make 22. Sew a remaining 2½" x 5" light rectangle to the remaining segments from step 1; press. Make 74. Each Pathways block will now measure 5" x 8½".

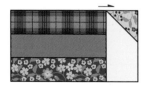

Make 22.

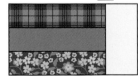

Make 74.

ASSEMBLING THE QUILT

1. Arrange the blocks in 12 vertical rows of 8 blocks each, offsetting the blocks in alternating rows by 4½" as shown and placing the 22 blocks with bar accent units as desired. Remove the blocks extending past the top edge of the layout, and trim 4" from the top of each one so the remaining block measures 5" x 4½". Replace the trimmed blocks in the layout. Remove the blocks extending past the bottom edge of the layout and trim 4" from the bottom of each one so the remaining block measures 5" x 4½". Replace these blocks in the layout.

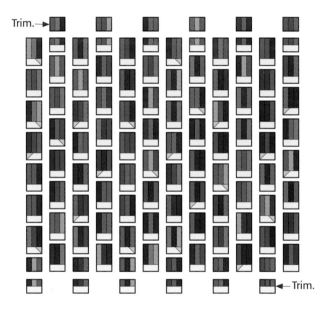

Trim.→   ←Trim.

2. Stitch the blocks in each vertical row together; press. Stitch the rows together to form the pieced quilt center as shown; press.

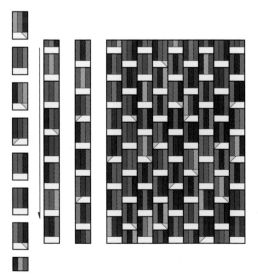

ADDING THE BORDERS

Refer to "Adding a Straight Border" on page 106 as needed to measure, join and/or trim, and sew the 2½"-wide inner-border strips and 5½"-wide outer-border strips to the quilt.

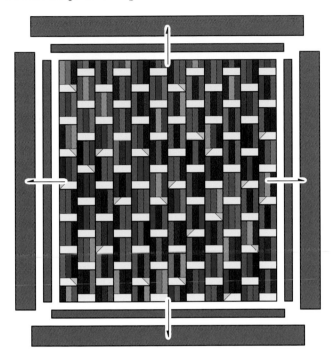

Hide treasure in a quilt pocket. See page 110 for ideas.

FINISHING THE QUILT

1. Refer to "Quilting Basics" on page 104 as needed to finish your quilt. Prepare the quilt backing, and then layer and baste together the backing, batting, and quilt top.

2. Quilt as desired. In the pictured quilt, we chose a medium-scale allover stipple or meander pattern.

3. Trim the excess batting and backing fabric, remove the basting, and use the 2½"-wide strips to bind your quilt.

4. Add a hanging sleeve, label, or pocket to your quilt, if desired. Refer to "Finishing Touches" on page 109 for methods, tips, and ideas.

Pathways Quilt
in reproduction fabrics

By Anne Moscicki and Linda Wyckoff-Hickey, 68" x 74". Quilted by Celeste Marshall.

Soft and sweet reproduction prints bring out the tender side of this easy quilt.

Make It with Friends!
Pathways Quilt Variation

This batik variation of the Pathways Quilt (68" x 74") was made at one of our annual beach retreats to donate to a community auction. Designed by Anne Moscicki and Linda Wyckoff-Hickey, 2002. Pieced by Denise Bohbot, Joan Croome, Laura Evans, Deb Hollister, Margie Keck Smith, Linda Kenney, Kyle McAvoy, Anne Moscicki, Maureen Reynolds, Mimi Teters, Julia Teters-Zeigler, Cora Tunberg, and Linda Wyckoff-Hickey. Quilted by Celeste Marshall.

This pattern divides easily for a group of eight people, with each participant making 12 blocks (see "Coordinating a Successful Group Quilt" on page 25). Note that this group variation does not include the bar accents you see in the basic Pathways pattern.

Select a fabric group to specify for use in the quilt. You'll need 24 different fat quarters or 228 scraps measuring at least 2" x 6½" in a wide variety of prints.

Purchase 1⅜ yards of fabric for the bar strip at the top of each block. Cut eight strips, 5" x 40", and distribute one to each participant, along with a request for additional fabrics from the chosen fabric group to be used for borders, backing, or binding for the finished quilt. Instructions for each participant follow, addressing usage of both yardage and scraps.

From yardage:

- Choose three ¼-yard pieces of fabric from the specified fabric group. From each piece, cut 2 strips, 2" x 40".
- Arrange the strips into two sets of three strips each, varying the fabric position in each set.
- Sew each set of three strips together to form a strip set (two total); press the seams open.
- Cut each strip set into six segments, 6½" wide (12 total).
- From the 5" x 40" strip of bar fabric, cut 12 rectangles, 2½" x 5". Sew one rectangle to the top of each strip-set segment. Each block will now measure 5" x 8½"; square up each block!
- Make 12 blocks.

From scraps:

- Select 36 scraps from the specified fabric group.
- Trim each scrap into a 2" x 6½" strip.
- Arrange the strips randomly into sets of three.
- Sew each set of three strips together to make a block. Make 12 blocks.
- From the 5" x 40" strip of bar fabric, cut 12 rectangles, 2½" x 5". Sew one rectangle to the top of each block. Each block will now measure 5" x 8½"; square up each block!
- Make 12 blocks.

Follow the directions and illustrations for the Pathways Quilt on pages 23–23 to assemble the blocks and borders and finish the quilt.

Coordinating a Successful Group Quilt

Pulling off a terrific group quilt is a lot like throwing a terrific party. Your guest list is composed of a group of quilters linked by a united purpose: generous hearts for a charity or community quilt, shared memories for a legacy quilt, a celebration of love for a wedding quilt, a vision of a bright future for a new baby's quilt, a warm hug for a sick friend's quilt.

Make each person's participation official in some tangible way, whether by email, letter, or postcard, and ask her or him to RSVP to confirm. Even the kindest of hearts needs a deadline, so set a date for blocks to be finished and delivered, and a time and place to assemble them into a quilt top. This is your opportunity to ask for donations of money, materials, or time for finishing the quilt, if required.

Coordinate the event with a pattern to suit the skill level of all the participants. The Pathways Quilt on page 19 and the Fluttering By Quilt and Pillow on page 28 are wonderful group patterns; even a brand-new quilter can create the blocks with just a bit of rotary-cutting advice. Gather a group of nonquilters and discuss ways to personalize the simple blocks for the Baby Love Quilt on page 40. Blocks that require matching seams, templates, or triangles require the participation of quilters with a bit more skill.

Play out the theme in the choice of fabrics, colors, and character of print. When describing fabric choices, use broadly descriptive words that evoke colors, moods, themes, and fabric groups, as well as whether you're expecting flannels, homespun, or flat goods. Consider sending everyone a swatch of fabric to use as a starting point in coordinating fabrics for his or her blocks.

The result? Laughter and conversation, of course, along with the joyous sense of belonging to a creative, sharing community…and a beautiful quilt to show for it!

Please note that the right to copy and distribute any of the text or designs in any book belongs to the publisher, and you must contact the publisher for permission each time you wish to copy material. As the owner of this book, you may make photocopies of the designs for ease of use in your personal projects, including gifts and nonprofit fundraising efforts of fewer than five quilts or projects. Copying any portion of this book to give away or to sell without written permission from Martingale & Company is not allowed by copyright laws. The publisher invites your inquiries; please email them at info@martingale-pub.com. For more information on copyright law, you can visit www.copyright.gov.

Alberta and Richard

*by Anne Moscicki and
Linda Wyckoff-Hickey, 14" x 14".*

Vivian and Rags

*by Anne Moscicki and
Linda Wyckoff-Hickey, 15" x 15".*

Jack and His Buddy

*by Anne Moscicki and
Linda Wyckoff-Hickey, 12" x 14".*

Yvonne

*by Anne Moscicki and
Linda Wyckoff-Hickey, 14" x 14".*

Too often, special photos are tucked away into albums. However, as the focal point of a beautiful pillow, these wonderful photos blend the past with the present, giving you the opportunity to enjoy them every day. Children, especially, love to hear that they come from families possessed of compassion, kindness, heroism, wisdom, humor, or ambition... though sometimes we all need a reminder that those traits exist in our family tree, if it is shaken hard enough! These pillows are sure to start those conversations.

—Anne and Linda

PICTURE PERFECT: WORKING WITH PHOTOS

Your treasured photographs deserve a unique setting, embracing a wide array of techniques to bring the best of your past into your everyday life. Gather up the fabrics, ribbons, beads, buttons, and charms that you love and start playing with them, adding and subtracting elements until you've found a combination that suits your style. Refer to "Tips and Techniques for Decorative Stitching" on page 50, "Letter Perfect: Creating Distinctive Monograms" on page 54, and "All Tied Up! Working with Ribbon" on page 67 for more ideas. When you have made the pillow top, measure it and follow the steps for completing the pillow using one of the methods described throughout the book.

- Check your local business directory for companies that restore antique photos if necessary.

- Choose the best type of fabric for printing your photograph. Different fabric weights, shades, and finishes are available, some with the option of ironing the image into place. Ask at your local quilt shop or browse online to research the choices.

- If you're a techno-quilter yourself or have a technologically oriented friend or family member, you may be able to scan, adjust color and tonal balance, and print the photograph onto quilting fabric right at home. If not, use the services of your local full-service copy shop or a photo-transfer business. Ask for referrals from your local quilt shop, or look online or in your local phone directory.

- Study the colors in your transferred photograph carefully before choosing fabrics for the pillow. Memory is a powerful thing, and you might know that your grandmother's dress was brilliant green, but the effects of age and the reproduction techniques that you used to transfer your photo to fabric may have dulled the color. Despite the clarity of the image in your memory, choose fabrics to complement the printed photo. Select fabrics with no tones darker than the deepest shadow area, or brighter than the lightest highlights, to bring out the best in the photograph.

FLUTTERING BY QUILT AND PILLOW

The inspiration for this quilt came from my daughter, Catherine, who wanted to learn to quilt along with her friends. We planned a retreat weekend where all the mothers passed along their pleasure in quilting. In turn, the girls chose to pass on the bright quilt they made to a children's charity. How extraordinary—and yet perfectly ordinary—to see these girls look out onto the world with the confidence that they will be able to give it a kinder shape.

—Anne

Materials

Yardage is based on 42"-wide fabric unless otherwise noted.

QUILT

2 yards of fabric for outer border and binding

½ yard of fabric for inner border

⅜ yard *each* of 10 assorted fabrics for blocks

6 fat quarters of assorted fabrics for appliqué wings

1 fat quarter of fabric for appliqué butterfly bodies

3¾ yards of fabric for backing

60" x 66" piece of batting

1 yard of fusible web

8½" square ruler

Assorted beads and buttons for embellishment (optional)

Embroidery floss for embellishment (optional)

PILLOW

½ yard of fabric for border

30 assorted scraps, each 2½" x 10½", for blocks

Fat quarters of 2 different fabrics for appliqué wings

1 fat quarter of fabric for appliqué butterfly bodies

⅞ yard of fabric for lining

¾ yard of fabric for backing

⅜ yard of fabric for binding

26" x 34" piece of batting

1 bed-sized pillow

½ yard of fusible web

8½" square ruler

Assorted beads and buttons for embellishment (optional)

Embroidery floss for embellishment (optional)

Fluttering By Quilt

By Anne Moscicki and Linda Wyckoff-Hickey, 54" x 60".
Inspired by Catherine Moscicki. Quilted by Amy Helmkamp.

CUTTING

Cut all strips from the crosswise grain unless otherwise noted.

QUILT

From *each* assorted ⅜-yard piece, cut:

◆ 4 strips, 2½" x 40"; subcut each strip into 3 strips, 2½" x 10½" (120 total)

From the inner-border fabric, cut:

◆ 5 strips, 2½" x 40"

From the *lengthwise grain* of the outer-border and binding fabric, cut:

◆ 3 strips, 4½" x 70"
◆ 1 strip, 14½" x 70"
◆ 4 strips, 2½" x 70"

PILLOW

From the border fabric, cut:

◆ 3 strips, 2½" x 40"

From the binding, cut:

◆ 3 strips, 2½" x 40"

From the lining, cut:

◆ 1 piece, 24" x 32"

From the backing, cut:

◆ 2 pieces, 20" x 23"

MAKING THE QUILT BLOCKS

1. Arrange five assorted 2½" x 10½" strips and sew them together along the long edges to make a 10½" square as shown. Press the seam allowances open. Make 24, varying the fabrics and fabric placement as much as possible.

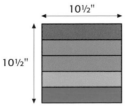

Make 24.

2. Angle an 8½" square ruler over each unit from step 1 and cut one block. Vary the placement of your ruler, cutting half the blocks tipped to the left and half the blocks tipped to the right as shown. Make 24.

Tipped left   Tipped right

ASSEMBLING THE QUILT

Referring to the quilt photo on page 30 and the illustration that follows, lay out the blocks in six horizontal rows of four blocks each. When you are pleased with the arrangement, sew the blocks together into rows. Press the seams open. Sew the rows together. Press the seams open.

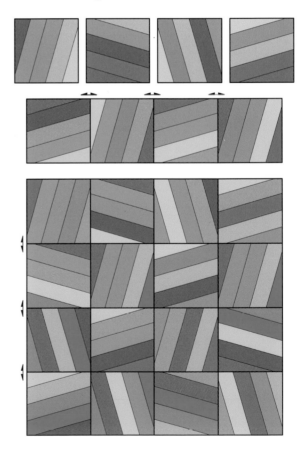

ADDING THE BORDERS

Refer to "Adding a Straight Border" on page 106 as needed to measure, join and/or trim, and sew the 2½"-wide inner-border strips to the sides, top, and bottom of the quilt; one 4½"-wide outer-border strip to the left side of the quilt; the 14½"-wide outer-border strip to the right side of the quilt; and the remaining 4½"-wide outer-border strips to the top and bottom.

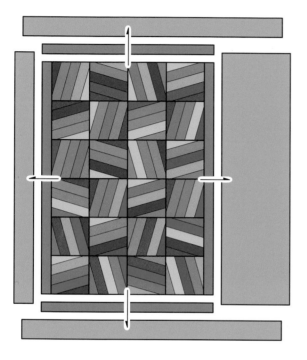

ADDING THE APPLIQUÉS

You will need six butterfly appliqués for the quilt. We chose a pinked edge for the butterfly wing appliqués, but made the butterfly bodies in the more traditional manner.

1. Use the patterns on page 35 and paper or template material to make templates for the butterfly body and wing shapes. Use the wing templates to trace butterfly wing pieces for six butterflies onto the paper side of the fusible web. Cut on the traced line with regular scissors.

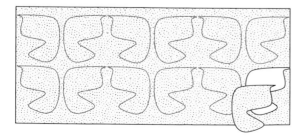

2. Press the wing shapes, paper side up, onto the wrong side of the wing fabric, leaving approximately ½" between the shapes and using heat and pressure according to the manufacturer's instructions. Use pinking shears to trim the fabric slightly (approximately ⅛") outside the edge of the fusible web. This gives the butterfly wings a little bit of a ruffled edge.

3. Use the body template to trace body pieces for six butterflies onto the paper side of the fusible web, leaving about ½" of space between the shapes. Cut out the shapes with regular scissors, leaving about ¼" around each shape. Press the body shapes, paper side up, onto the wrong side of the body fabric, and cut out the shapes on the traced line.

4. Referring to the project photo on page 30 and the diagram below for suggested appliqué placement, fuse the butterfly wings and bodies to the quilt. You may choose to secure all appliqué pieces with a machine straight stitch as we did, or substitute your own favorite stitch. Refer to "Tips and Techniques for Decorative Stitching" on page 50 for tips and inspiration.

Finishing the Quilt

1. Refer to "Quilting Basics" on page 104 as needed to finish your quilt. Prepare the quilt backing, and then layer and baste together the backing, batting, and quilt top.

2. Quilt as desired. For this project we chose free-form swirls that accentuate the suggested movement of the butterflies.

3. Trim the excess batting and backing fabric, remove the basting, and use the 2½"-wide strips to bind your quilt.

4. Add a hanging sleeve, label, or pocket to your quilt, if desired. Refer to "Finishing Touches" on page 109 for methods, tips, and ideas.

5. Add buttons, beads, embroidery, or other embellishments as desired.

Fluttering By Pillow

*By Anne Moscicki and
Linda Wyckoff-Hickey,
30½" x 22½".*

*Inspired by Catherine Moscicki.
Quilted by Amy Helmkamp.*

Making the Pillow

1. Referring to "Making the Quilt Blocks" on page 31, make six blocks using the assorted 2½" x 10½" strips.

2. Referring to the diagram that follows, lay out the blocks in two horizontal rows of three blocks each. When you are pleased with the arrangement, sew the blocks together into rows. Press the seams open. Sew the rows together. Press the seams open.

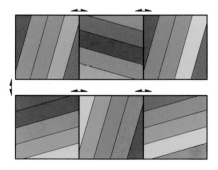

3. Refer to "Adding a Straight Border" on page 106 as needed to measure, join and/or trim, and sew the 2½"-wide border strips to the sides, top, and bottom of the pillow top. Press the seam allowances to the outer edges.

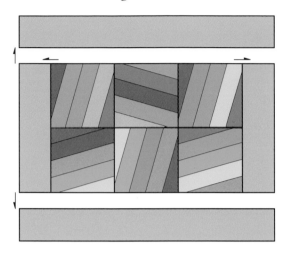

4. Refer to "Adding the Appliqués" on page 32 and the diagram that follows to appliqué two butterflies to the pillow top.

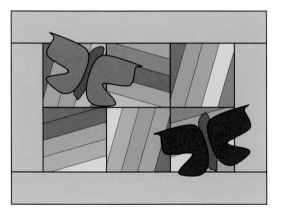

5. Refer to "Quilting Basics" on page 104 as necessary. Layer the pieced pillow top, batting, and lining fabric; baste. Quilt as desired. Trim the excess batting and lining even with the pillow top.

6. Fold one 20" edge of a pillow backing piece over 2" to the wrong side, resulting in an 18" x 23" piece; press. Make a row of stitching next to the fold to secure and finish it as shown. Add

two more rows of stitching ¼" from the folded raw edge. Repeat to prepare the second backing piece.

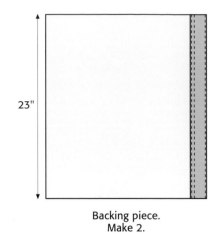

Backing piece.
Make 2.

7. Place the quilted pillow top, wrong side up, on a clean, flat workspace. Layer one backing piece, right side up, over the quilted pillow top, aligning the raw edges. Place the second backing piece, aligning the raw edges. (The backing pieces will overlap.) Pin all the layers.

Overlap

8. Turn the unit over. Refer to "Adding the Binding" on page 108 as needed to bind the pillow edges using the 2½"-wide binding strips. Add buttons, beads, embroidery, or other embellishments; insert a pillow, and you're finished!

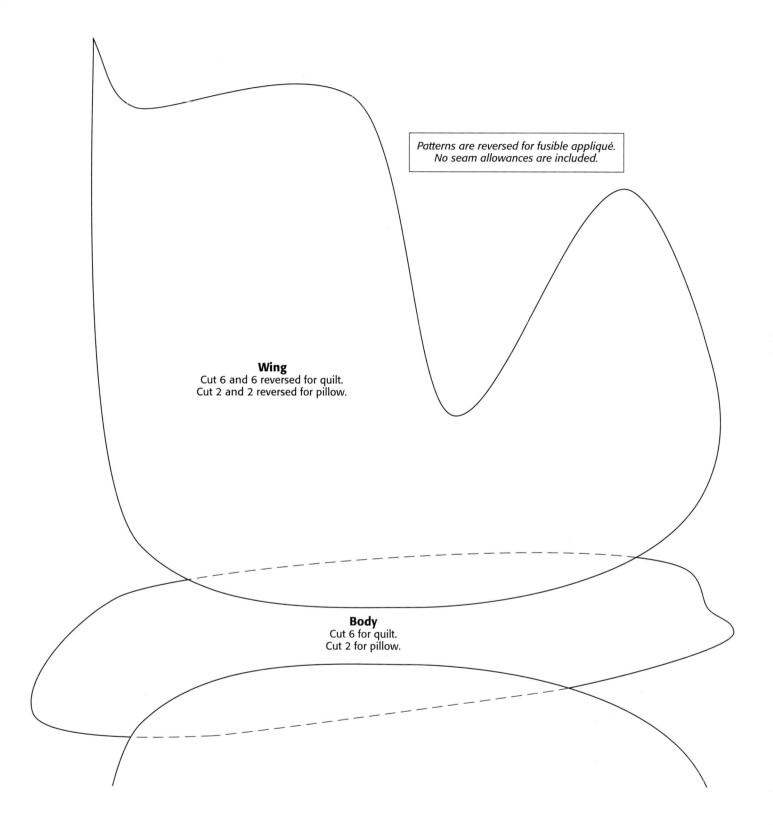

Patterns are reversed for fusible appliqué.
No seam allowances are included.

Wing
Cut 6 and 6 reversed for quilt.
Cut 2 and 2 reversed for pillow.

Body
Cut 6 for quilt.
Cut 2 for pillow.

DOWN BY THE BAY
QUILT AND PILLOW

By Anne Moscicki and Linda Wyckoff-Hickey, 54" x 60".
Inspired by Catherine Moscicki. Quilted by Celeste Marshall.

C'mon in, the water's fine! To make this "finny" variation, follow the Fluttering By instructions on pages 29–34 and use the appliqué fabrics, appliqué directions, and quilting suggestions that follow. Dive into a batch of fat quarters as you choose fabrics for your quilted aquarium: will your fish be graceful river trout, splashy goldfish, or jewels of an exotic coral reef?

FISH APPLIQUÉ MATERIALS

QUILT

12 fat eighths of assorted fabrics *or* scraps at least 4" x 16", for fish bodies

6 assorted scraps, 3" x 5", for fish tails

Fat eighth of red fabric for fish lips

Buttons for eyes

PILLOW

4 fat eighths of assorted fabrics *or* scraps at least 4" x 16", for fish bodies

2 scraps, 3" x 5", for fish tails

Fat eighth of red fabric for fish lips

Buttons for eyes

ADDING THE APPLIQUÉS, STITCHING, AND EMBELLISHMENT

1. Use the patterns on pages 38–39 and paper or template material to make templates for the fish body (two pieces), tail, and lip shapes. Note that one fish is swimming in the opposite direction on the pillow; simply reverse the templates to make that fish if you desire.

2. Use the templates to trace pieces for the appropriate number of fish (six for the quilt, two for the pillow) onto the paper side of the fusible web,

leaving about ½" of space between the shapes. Cut out the shapes with regular scissors, leaving about ¼" around each shape. Press the shapes, paper side up, onto the wrong side of the appropriate fabrics, and cut out the shapes on the traced line.

3. Refer to the illustrations that follow for suggested appliqué placement, and fuse the fish in place. Use your favorite decorative stitch to secure the appliqué edges, referring to "Tips and Techniques for Decorative Stitching" on page 50 for inspiration. The button eyes are hand stitched in place after quilting. If you like, you can layer buttons of different colors and sizes for dimension and whimsy.

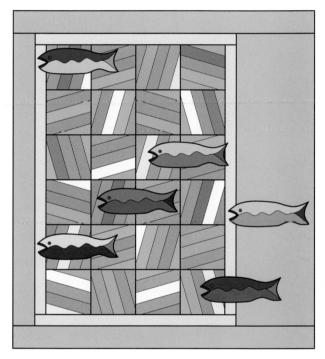

Quilt plan

Pillow plan

QUILTING

Quilt as desired. For the project shown we chose watery swirls that accentuate the forward motion of the school of fish.

Cut 6 of each piece for quilt.
Cut 1 and 1 reversed of each piece for pillow.
Patterns are reversed for fusible appliqué.
No seam allowances are included.

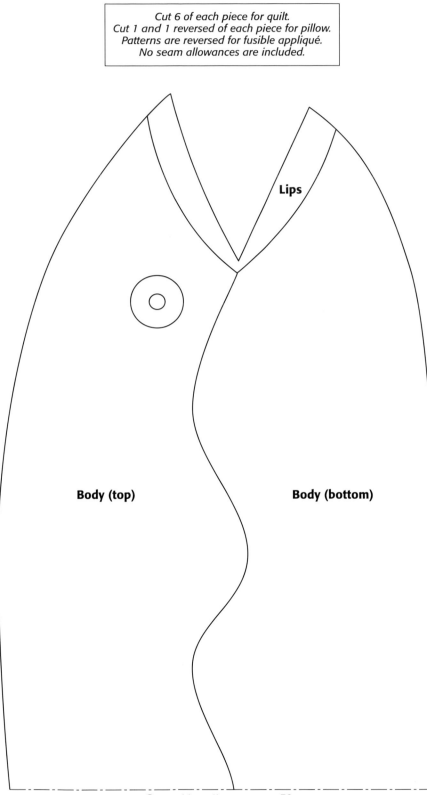

Lips

Body (top)

Body (bottom)

Connect to pattern on page 39.

Connect to pattern on page 38.

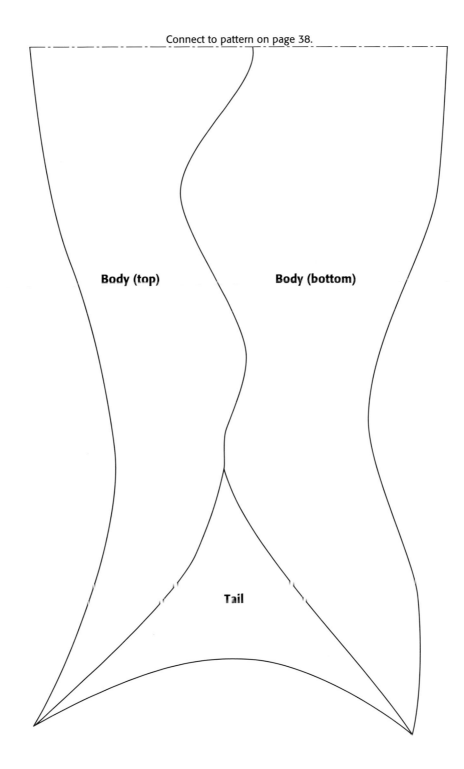

Body (top)

Body (bottom)

Tail

BABY LOVE QUILT

Living far away from family and friends, I've made and mailed many a baby quilt! When I finally have the opportunity to meet the new arrival, sometimes years later, the truest reward is to find myself warmly welcomed with "I know you! You're the Aunt Linda that made my quilt!" Bring your family and friends into the circle of love surrounding a new life by asking them to share in making this special quilt.

—Linda

MATERIALS

Yardage is based on 42"-wide fabric unless otherwise noted.

2½ yards of fabric for border and binding

1⅛ yards of light fabric for large hearts

⅞ yard of contrasting fabric for small hearts

1 square, 10" x 10", of white fabric for center block

25 squares, 8½" x 8½", of assorted prints for block backgrounds

3½ yards of fabric for backing

62" x 62" piece of batting

6 yards of 1"-wide ribbon to frame the center block and pieced quilt center

2 yards of fusible web

Pinking shears or other decorative-edged scissors

Permanent fabric-marking pens, embroidery supplies, or other materials to personalize the blocks

CUTTING

From the *lengthwise grain* of the border and binding fabric, cut:

◆ 4 strips, 8½" x 60"

From the *crosswise grain* of the remaining border and binding fabric, cut:

◆ 6 strips, 2½" x 40"

MAKING THE BABY LOVE BLOCKS

1. Use the patterns on page 45 and paper or template material to make templates for the large and small heart shapes. Use the templates to trace 24 small hearts and 24 large hearts onto the fusible web.

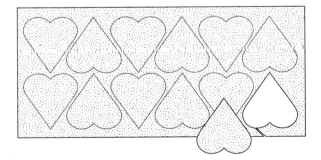

Baby Love Quilt

By Anne Moscicki and Linda Wyckoff-Hickey, 56" x 56".

Quilted by Celeste Marshall.

2. Press the small heart shapes, paper side up, to the wrong side of the small heart fabric, leaving approximately ½" between the shapes and using heat and pressure according to the manufacturer's instructions. Use pinking shears to trim the fabric slightly outside the edge of the fusible web.

3. Repeat step 2 using the shapes and fabric for the large hearts.

4. Lay out the assorted 8½" squares in five rows of five squares each, arranging the colors and patterns in a pleasing way. Refer to the quilt plan on page 44 to identify the two blocks each in rows 1, 2, 4, and 5 with diagonally placed hearts. Working one block at a time, remove each of these blocks from the layout. Remove the paper backing from one large heart and diagonally center the shape on the 8½" square. Remove the paper backing from one small heart and center it on top of the large heart. Fuse the layers together and return the block to the layout. Make eight blocks with diagonally centered hearts.

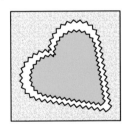

Make 8.

5. Repeat step 4 to make 16 blocks with the hearts centered vertically on the 8½" square.

Make 16.

6. Stitch around both heart shapes on each block, about ⅛" inside the pinked edges. We used a straight stitch on the large hearts and a decorative stitch on the small hearts. See "Tips and Techniques for Decorative Stitching" on page 50 for tips and inspiration.

MAKING THE CENTER BLOCK

1. Trace and cut one 5½" square from fusible web. Fuse the square, paper side up, roughly in the center of the wrong side of the 10" white square.

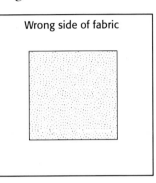

2. Staying within the fused area, embellish the front of the white square as desired. You might include the newcomer's name and birth date, a monogram, a meaningful verse, or a gentle nursery rhyme. Refer to "Letter Perfect: Creating Distinctive Monograms" on page 54 for inspiration and tips to create a look similar to our quilt shown on page 42.

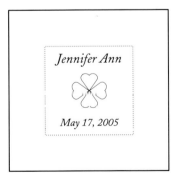

3. Use pinking shears to trim the embellished white square ⅛" outside the edge of the fusible web.

4. Center the embellished square on the remaining 8½" square and fuse it in place. Arrange a piece of ribbon ⅛" outside the edges of the pinked square, mitering the ribbon corners. Secure the ribbon to the square with a straight stitch just inside the ribbon edges on both sides. Refer to "All Tied Up! Working with Ribbon" on page 67 for additional tips and inspiration. Return the block to its position in the layout.

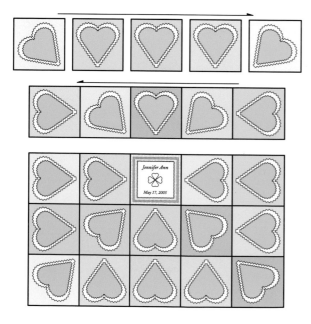

ASSEMBLING THE QUILT

Stitch the blocks together into rows; press. Stitch the rows together, matching the block seams. Press the seam allowances to one side.

ADDING THE BORDER

1. Refer to "Adding a Mitered Border" on page 106 as needed to measure, join and/or trim, and sew the 8½"-wide border to the quilt, mitering the corners.

2. Pin the remaining ribbon ¼" from the seam between the pieced quilt center and the border, mitering the ribbon corners. Secure the ribbon to the quilt with a straight stitch just inside the ribbon edges on both sides. Stitch the mitered corner down by hand or machine.

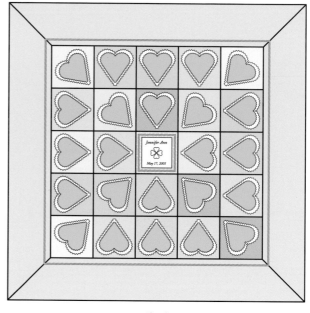

Quilt plan

FINISHING THE QUILT

1. Refer to "Quilting Basics" on page 104 as needed to finish your quilt. Prepare the quilt backing, and then layer and baste together the backing, batting, and quilt top.

2. Quilt as desired. In the pictured quilt, the background squares were quilted with a leaf-and-vine motif, and the unembellished areas of the center block were filled with a micro-stipple or meander pattern. A stylized leaf-and-floral design encircles the quilt in the outer border.

3. Trim the excess batting and backing fabric, remove the basting, and use the 2½"-wide strips to bind your quilt.

4. Add a hanging sleeve, label, or pocket to your quilt, if desired. Refer to "Finishing Touches" on page 109 for methods, tips, and ideas.

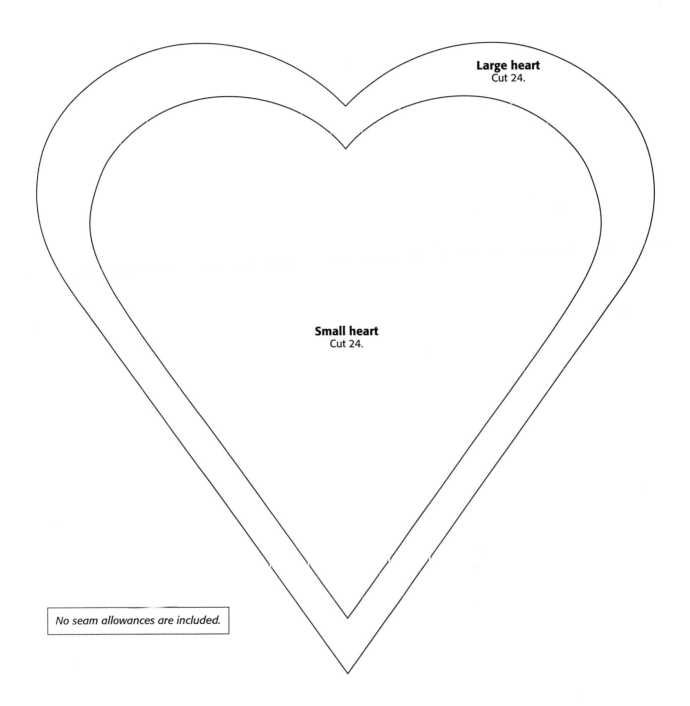

Large heart
Cut 24.

Small heart
Cut 24.

No seam allowances are included.

Make It with Friends!
Baby Love Quilt Variation

Baby Love Quilts

Designed by Anne Moscicki and Linda Wyckoff-Hickey, 40" x 40". Pieced by Judy A. Eriksen, Margaret H. Hayes, Maureen S. Healy Funk, Linda L. Hoag, Kathy Koning, W. R. Mahorney, Linda McLaughlin, Anne Moscicki, Elvira Olinger, Gail Y. O'Toole, Cindy Pope, Mimi Teters, Tracy Robinson, Patricia A. Shehane, Leslie A. Vilendre, Kathy Wheatley, and Linda Wyckoff-Hickey. Quilted by Celeste Marshall.

The Baby Love Quilt makes an excellent project for a group gift to a much-anticipated little one. Include nonquilters in the creative process by precutting the center hearts and offering them to shower guests or by mail to faraway friends and family members to inscribe with their personal

welcome-to-this-world messages. For more tips and ideas, see "Coordinating a Successful Group Quilt" on page 25.

This variation is divided for a group of 12 participants, with each participant making two blocks.

Note that this group variation does not include the borders you see in the basic Baby Love Quilt pattern.

To coordinate this quilt you will need:

- 1⅛ yards of white fabric, cut into 24 squares, 7" x 7", for the small center hearts. Distribute two squares to each participant.
- ½ yard of fabric for binding
- 2⅝ yards of fabric for backing
- 46" x 46" piece of batting

In addition to the two 7" x 7" squares of white fabric, each participant will need:

- 18" x 18" piece of fusible web
- 2 fat quarters of reproduction fabric for the large hearts and background squares
- Pinking shears
- Permanent fabric-marking pens

Assign four participants to produce two diagonally oriented heart blocks each; the remaining eight participants will each make two vertically oriented heart blocks. Assign one person to assemble the fabric for and create the center block.

Follow the directions and illustrations for the Baby Love Quilt on pages 41–44 to assemble the blocks and complete the quilt.

--- TIP ---

The rhythmic curves of rickrack recall the simplicity and playfulness of childhood, making a perfect addition to a child's quilt. And it's so easy!

Lightly press the rickrack to flatten it. Pin it into place. Stitch down the center of the rickrack to secure it to the base fabric. Stitch the rickrack twice again, catching the tops of the rounded edges to keep them neatly in place.

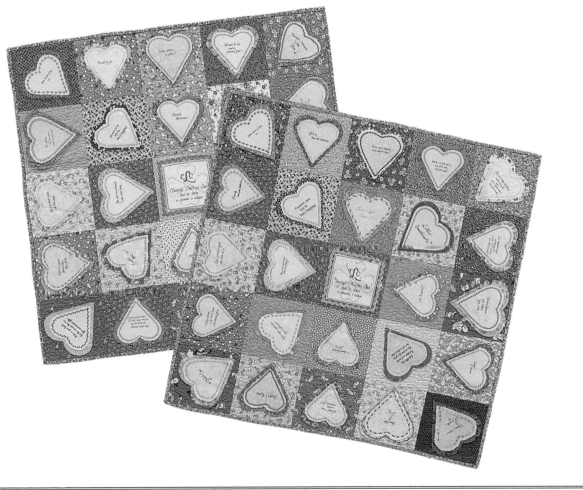

Make It Simple! Quick-Turn Quilt

Designed by Kathy Wheatley, 32" x 52".
Made by Anne Moscicki, Philip Hickey, and Linda Wyckoff-Hickey.

Many organizations across the country create quilts to comfort children in crisis, and sadly, demand always outstrips the supply. Kathy Wheatley, founder of Comforting Kids Network/Quilts For Kids in Lake Oswego, Oregon, shares her pattern for this "Quick-Turn Quilt," the simplest snuggly quilt we've ever seen. The cheerful prints, bright colors, and warm textures of the fabrics make these quilts special, but there's an extra, intangible element the quilters often add: their meditations and prayers as they create these thoughtful gifts.

These little quilts are a great way to develop machine-quilting skills on a manageable scale. The method is simple enough that you can involve your children in helping other children while you pass on your love of quilting.

MATERIALS

Yardage is based on 42"-wide fabric.

1½ yards *each* of 2 fabrics that would appeal to a child; Kathy has found, in her experience with donated quilts, that even teenagers often choose fabrics that would appeal to much younger children.

44" x 58" piece of batting

Note: The exact finished size of your quilt may vary slightly depending on the degree of shrinkage in your fabrics.

Making the Quilt

1. Remove the selvages from each 1½-yard piece of fabric. Trim the fabric pieces so that they are the same size; press.

2. Smooth the batting onto a clean, flat workspace. Layer one piece of trimmed fabric right side up on top of the batting. The batting should extend slightly beyond the edge of the fabric on all sides.

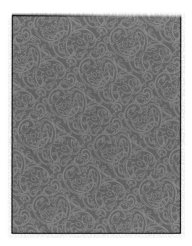

3. Layer the second piece of trimmed fabric wrong side up over the other two layers, aligning the fabric edges. Use a few pins on each side to hold the layers in place. Double-pin in two places on one long side, placing the pins 10" apart.

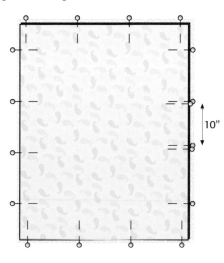

4. Stitch the layers ½" from the fabric edges, beginning at one double-pinned spot and ending at the other to leave a 10" opening as shown.

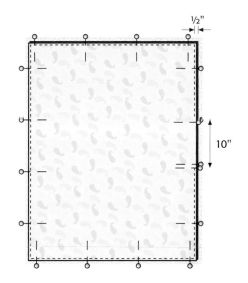

5. Clip the corners at a 45° angle. Turn the quilt right side out through the 10" opening so that the batting becomes the middle layer. Use a tool with a blunt tip, such as a chopstick, to square the corners.

Finishing the Quilt

Whipstitch the opening closed. Machine stitch around all four sides a scant ¼" from the edge, and then again ½" from the edge. Secure the layers by hand quilting, tacking or tying, or by using your sewing maching to straight stitch, free-motion quilt, or repeat a single decorative stitch.

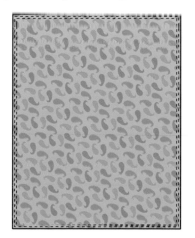

Tips and Techniques for Decorative Stitching

The quickest, least expensive, and most effective embellishment of all may be sitting right in front of you: the decorative stitches on your sewing machine. If you haven't tried them out, gather up some scraps and thread and schedule yourself a little playtime to get to know them! The beauty of even simple stitches can make a big impact in your finished project.

Decorative stitches can be used to define or echo a shape, as in our Baby Love Quilt on page 40. Or try creating rows of different stitches in different thread colors to anchor and enhance fusible-web appliqué, as we did in the Down by the Bay variation of our Fluttering By Quilt (see page 36). To add emphasis to a pieced quilt block, use decorative stitching along the edge of a pieced area, such as a star shape, using your ¼" foot as a guide. Add a garland of decorative stitching to a pieced inner border. Just about any project that needs a little "oomph!" can become your next opportunity to use decorative stitches.

- Start with a test piece that closely resembles your finished project—perhaps the leftover edges of fused fabrics ironed to a leftover background piece, or a trimmed edge of a layered project. This allows you to check the thread colors, adjust the tension, and practice the same curves or angles.

- Try using different stitches in different ways. A simple blanket stitch can easily anchor almost any appliqué, but if you turn the piece so that the stitches radiate from the appliqué center, stars will twinkle and flower centers will suddenly sprout!

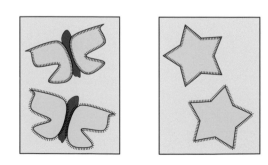

- Go slowly until you catch the rhythm of the particular stitch you've chosen.

- Different thread weights can add folk-art charm or sophisticated polish. Try them out on scraps to determine the effect that best suits your project.

- Experiment with different thread colors and shades to produce hard edges or soft shading in the finished piece. Add dimension by changing to a deeper, darker shade on the shadow side of a shape.

- Experiment with stitch width and length; be sure the foot will accommodate the needle position for your chosen stitch.

- Your sewing machine may allow you to change the needle position to the left or right. If so, adjust it to your advantage when stitching on embellishments such as ribbons, or to align edges of decorative stitches.

- As you round corners, rotate the entire piece, rather than just steering the edge into the sewing machine. Allow the feed dogs to advance the fabric as you gently guide it along.

- Count out the rhythm as the needle goes into the fabric in order to control your turns and corners. For example, in a leaf-and-flower stitch you will want to turn after a leaf is completed but before the flower begins.

- Choose a bobbin thread that matches the top thread to lessen the effects of show-through or shading to the top. Adjust the machine tension if necessary.

- Add a little stiffness to the fabrics with spray sizing, spray starch, or tear-away stabilizer. If the piece you're stitching will be joined to the quilt with fusible web, the web will provide stiffness. Different fusible products vary in weight and stiffness, so try a variety to find the best option for each project.

- Pull thread ends through to the back of the quilt top to finish seams.

RING BEARER'S PILLOW

By Anne Moscicki and Linda Wyckoff-Hickey, 8" x 8" excluding scalloped edge.

The sheer organza ribbons on this heirloom pillow hold the traditional symbols of eternal love between bride and groom. Create the ruffled edge with gathered half circles of coordinating fabrics.

MATERIALS

Yardage is based on 42"-wide fabric.

⅜ yard of fabric for scalloped edge

2 squares, 8½" x 8½", of fabric for pillow-top background and backing

1 square, 7" x 7", of fabric for large heart

1 square, 6" x 6", of contrasting fabric for small heart

1¼ yards of lace

Scraps of fusible web

2 pieces, 20" long, of sheer ribbon for ring ties

Pillow stuffing

Scented additions for the stuffing, such as lavender for devotion, rosemary for loyalty, or sage for long life

MAKING THE PILLOW TOP

If you wish to add a monogram, dates, photograph, or other embellishment to the small center heart, do so before assembling the block.

1. Referring to "Making the Baby Love Blocks" on page 41, create a layered and appliquéd heart block using one 8½" fabric square and the 7" and 6" fabric squares.

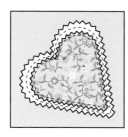

2. With raw edges aligned and right sides together, pin the lace all around the perimeter of the block. Baste the lace in place using a straight or zigzag stitch, mitering the corners and stitching a scant ¼" from the edge of the block.

MAKING THE SCALLOPED EDGE

1. Cut two strips, 5" x 42", from the fabric for the scalloped edge. Fold each strip in half wrong side out to 5" x 21"; press.

2. Use the pattern on page 53 and paper or template material to make a template for the pillow scallop. Use the template to trace 10 scallop shapes onto each folded strip from step 1 as shown. Pin each scallop shape and cut out each scallop pair on the drawn line.

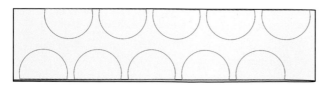

3. Stitch ¼" from the curved edge of each scallop pair as shown. Clip the curved edge of the seam allowance, and turn the scallop right side out; press. Make 20 scallops.

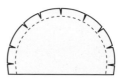

ASSEMBLING THE PILLOW

1. Lengthen the straight stitch on your sewing machine (to a long basting stitch, for example) and stitch across the straight edge of each scallop a scant ¼" from the raw edge as shown. Use threads of different colors in the needle and the bobbin so the threads will be easier to identify as you gather the scallops.

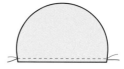

2. Pull the bobbin thread to gather the scallops to approximately 1½" wide as shown.

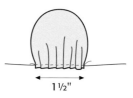

1½"

3. Arrange five gathered scallops along one edge of the lace-trimmed block, aligning the raw edges and leaving ¼" free of scallops at each end. Pin the scallops securely and use a walking foot to stitch them to the block a scant ¼" from the edge. Repeat to add five scallops to each remaining side.

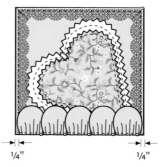
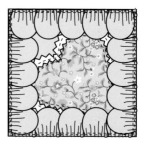

¼"   ¼"

4. Fold the ribbons in half lengthwise and secure them to the top point of the heart with a few hand stitches as shown. Gather the ribbons in the center of the block and pin gently to hold them away from the block edges as you add the pillow backing.

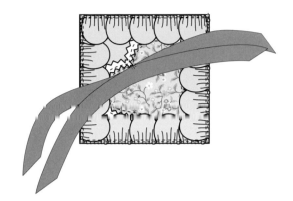

5. Place the remaining 8½" fabric square right sides together over the pillow top, aligning the raw edges. Use the walking foot on your sewing machine to stitch ¼" from the edge, leaving a 4" opening.

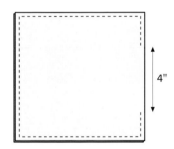

6. Turn the pillow right side out through the opening. Add the stuffing and scents, and whipstitch the opening closed. Tie on the wedding bands, and you're ready to walk down the aisle!

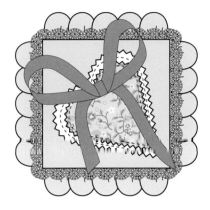

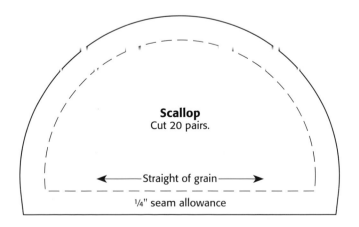

Scallop
Cut 20 pairs.

←— Straight of grain —→

¼" seam allowance

Letter Perfect: Creating Distinctive Monograms

At one time, monograms were instantly recognizable symbols of royal authority. Today, monograms still evoke an aura of sophistication, adaptable to any number of projects and an endless range of styles, from playful to chic, retro-funky to classically elegant. Quilters of any skill level can have fun adding monograms with the wide variety of techniques available, such as permanent fabric-marking pens, transfers, computer-printed fabric, fusible-web appliqué, embroidery, machine stitching, and endless combinations of these mediums.

The centerpiece of a monogram is the typography. Some basic styles are shown below.

Ll
Serif.
A serif is the small crossbar at the end of each stroke. These typefaces come in many styles, from blocky squares to graceful tapers.

Ll
Sans serif.
Clean and modern, sans serif typefaces may also have varying stroke weights.

Ll
Roman.
Roman type has primarily horizontal and vertical strokes, and may be serif or sans serif.

Ll
Italic.
Many roman typefaces have an italicized counterpart.

Ll
Script.
Flowing strokes can evoke either formal elegance or the casual air of handwriting.

Consider letter styles that express the personality you want to convey: playful, sophisticated, bold, elegant, whimsical, classic, or funky. As you look for letterforms, think about how you will reproduce the monogram onto fabric:

• Permanent fabric-marking pens are a good choice for delicate lines and swashes.

• Fusible-web appliqué is best suited to thick letters in larger sizes and with sharp, square serifs.

• Embroidery nicely reproduces the delicate lines in script letters, or provides filler for thick letters, while adding appealing texture and a classic, heirloom look.

• Transfers and computer printing onto fabric allow you to combine a variety of elements and skills to produce your design.

Playful and unconventional. A good candidate for appliqué in larger sizes or for computer reproduction.

Casually elegant. Pens will capture the nuance of line weight; also a good choice for chain-stitched embroidery.

Sweet and old-fashioned, though may not be instantly recognizable as the letter *a*. Use pens or computer reproduction techniques.

Classic and dependable, the solid lines and thick, square serifs will reproduce well with fusible-web appliqué.

Adventurous and a bit rogueish, as if pulled off a pirate's map! Use pens to reproduce the uneven edges.

Sweeping and graceful. Use pens or very fine embroidery to reproduce its flowing character.

Formal and precise. Pens or embroidery will reproduce the outline; fill in the open areas with contrasting color to add punch.

Simple and fresh. The high contrast of thick and thin lines makes this a good option for computer reproduction.

Strong and solid. A good candidate for fusible-web appliqué. You could embellish these heavy lines with embroidery.

Popular for teen monograms and suitable for fusible web in large sizes. Try contrasting hand stitches to outline.

You can find beautiful letters in just about any printed material, from newspaper advertisements to the wide variety of copyright-free books available in libraries or bookstores. An array of decorative alphabets in sticker form can be found in craft stores and other sources of scrapbooking supplies. Photocopy these letters to enlarge or reduce to the size you want.

The hunt for the perfect letter may take you no farther than your own home computer (or one at the library or local copy shop that offers business services). The computer allows you to print a variety of typefaces and sizes to work with. Look for decorative headline fonts, and preview them in a basic word-processing program in a large size, such as 72-point. Many additional fonts are available to download free from Web sites, and even more—including many specialty fonts—are available for online purchase. See "Resources" on page 111.

Multiple-letter monograms take a bit more work. You'll need to find typefaces offering your required letters in a style that will nestle together beautifully. The results lend a feeling of luxury and sophistication that is well worth the hunt.

Also look for decorative touches to further carry out the mood of the monogram: a fern leaf to trace behind the letterforms, a wreath of flowers embroidered to surround them, or an antique bookplate motif printed onto fabric and fused into place to frame the letters.

Before applying any monogram to fabric, work it out completely with sketches or on your computer so that your time is spent enjoying the finished project, not ripping it apart!

FUSING MONOGRAMS

Fusible web works well only for typography in large sizes, with thick serifs or no serifs at all; refer to the examples on page 54. Decide on the size of the letters by gauging how comfortable you are stitching around the edges in your preferred method, that is, by hand or machine. Use the following method to transfer and fuse the monogram:

1. Trace or print the letter onto a sheet of paper.

2. Tape the paper to a light box or window with the *wrong side* toward you so that the backward letter shape is visible. Tape a piece of fusible web, paper side toward you, over the marked paper and trace the letter with a sharp pencil.

3. Follow the manufacturer's instructions to fuse the web to the back of the letter fabric. Use sharp scissors to cut out the letter directly on the traced line.

4. Fuse the shape to the fabric base. Stitch around the letter by hand or machine to secure the edges.

A machine buttonhole stitch anchors the edges of this fusible web monogram

EMBROIDERING MONOGRAMS

Basic embroidery stitches work beautifully for reproducing many letterforms. Though often thought of as time-consuming, embroidery is simple to learn and easy to transport to soccer practice or guild meetings. Embroidered monograms are often viewed as aristocratic and expensive—even stuffy!—but your choice of typography and stitches can bring out a whimsical side, too.

Just trace the letters onto the base fabric using your favorite marking tool. On light-colored fabric, try a hard-lead pencil, No. 4 or higher, and then stitch over the traced letters. For darker fabrics or on wool, use a light-colored, removable marking tool, such as tailor's chalk. Here are some additional tips and guidelines:

- Split multistrand floss to create fine lines.

- Select a needle with an eye that accommodates the number of strands of floss you plan to use, and in a width that pierces the fabric smoothly.

- Use a solid running stitch to create delicate swashes; fill in larger areas with satin stitches, outlining them with more solid running stitches to accentuate the flowing letterforms of script.

- Add homespun interest with buttonhole or broken running-stitch outlines.

- Use a chain stitch for simple script typography or handwriting.

- Use a French knot to dot the letter *i* or fill a letter with texture.

This block, from a quilt made by Anne's family, shows several styles of embroidered typography.

CREATING MONOGRAMS WITH WOOL STRIPS

Use wool strips to shape an initial in school-marm cursive, trimming the strips to size as you lay out each letter stroke. Pin each stroke sparsely at first, and then add pins as the letter takes the shape you

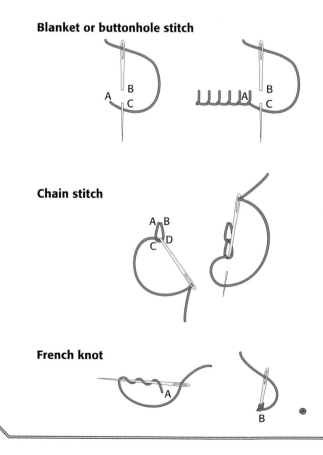

Blanket or buttonhole stitch

Chain stitch

French knot

Broken running stitch

Solid running stitch

Satin stitch

like. Pin the final shape securely and use a steam iron to smooth the shape into place. (Glass-head pins are handy for this technique.) Stitch the letterform in place by hand or machine.

The following example shows a letter made from ⅜"-wide wool strips. Each letter stroke was stitched separately, creating layers. Overlapping portions were turned aside to accommodate the stitching on a lower-layer stroke, and then pinned again for stitching.

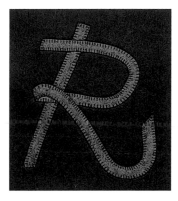

This letter is made from two wool strips stitched into place.

MONOGRAMMING WITH PERMANENT FABRIC-MARKING PENS

As easy and fun as the crayons of your childhood, pens offer lots of creative options for monogramming. They give you the ability to reproduce intricate designs: delicate script typefaces, scrolls, swashes, vines, and curlicues. Look online or in copyright-free design books for letterforms and motifs, or doodle your own. Consider yourself a painter with a link always there are no limits to your creative options! Here are some thoughts on selecting and using these versatile tools:

- If you haven't used permanent pens before, take a bit of time to experiment on a fabric scrap before you commit to your final piece.

- When shopping for pens, take a fabric scrap along so you can try before you buy; ask the shopkeeper for permission. Some manufacturers offer different pen tips in a variety of widths and colors; some inks bleed more easily than others; and some colors don't look exactly as the pen caps indicate.

- Experiment with washing, drying, and pressing your samples to see if and how this affects the color shade or intensity of the ink.

- Always work on a larger piece of fabric than you need, and trim to the necessary size when your design is complete.

- If you will be fusing the finished design, add fusible web to the back of the fabric first, and then trace or write. The web adds stiffness to the fabric, allowing you to reproduce the design more clearly and position it more precisely. Once you've completed the design, peel away the paper backing and fuse into place following the manufacturer's directions as usual.

- To trace a design, tape the design to a light box or bright window. Layer the fabric you'll be using over the design, position as desired using the translucence of the light source, and then tape and trace the lettering.

- Move the pen lightly over the surface of the fabric to avoid catching the weave of the cloth and to prevent the ink from bleeding across the fabric. The narrower the pen tip, the more easily it will catch in the weave.

- If a smooth, flowing line seems daunting, try tiny dots. Dots can also be used to fill in a small area, giving the impression of a lighter color shade.

- Consider mixing small dots of different colors to add depth or shadows to your design.

- Use small, light strokes to fill an area. Avoid overlapping, which may produce a mottled effect.

COMBINING TECHNIQUES

If you prefer, choose a combination of your favorite techniques, using different methods to create different typographical aspects of your project. For example:

- Create a large block-style letter with fusible web, and then embellish it by embroidering around the edges or stitching embroidered flowers in the center of the letter's thickest lines.

- Produce a beautiful script initial using a computer or a photo-transfer process, and surround it with ferns or flowers traced in pen from a copyright-free design book.

STAR PILLOWS

By Anne Moscicki and Linda Wyckoff-Hickey, approximately 18" x 18".

Since I live far away from many of the friends and family of my childhood, I have kept in touch and celebrated life's milestones via telephone, Christmas cards, emails, and the occasional handmade hug. These simple pillows are the perfect size for snuggling, and the pocket on the back is just the place to tuck a bedtime story, a tiny flashlight, wishes, dreams, or a special charm for the children you love.
—Linda

MATERIALS

2 squares, 22" x 22", of fabric for pillow top and backing

Pillow stuffing

Fabric for pocket (optional; see "Pocket Treasures" on page 110 for yardage guidelines)

If you plan to quilt one side of the pillow, you will also need:

22" x 22" piece of batting

22" x 22" square of muslin or lightweight scrap fabric for lining

MAKING THE PILLOW

1. If you are quilting one side of the pillow, refer to "Quilting Basics" on page 104 as needed. Layer one square of the pillow fabric right side up over the batting and the lining, baste. Quilt as desired.

2. Enlarge the pattern on page 60 by 300% to approximately 20" x 20". Use paper or template material to make a template.

3. Use the template to cut out a star from each 22" square of pillow fabric, whether quilted or not.

4. If you are adding a pocket, refer to "Pocket Treasures" on page 110 for methods, tips, and ideas. Center and stitch the pocket pieces on the right side of one star shape.

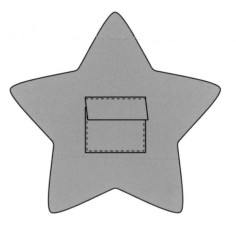

5. Layer the two star shapes, right sides together. Pin, and then stitch around the edges with a ¼" seam, leaving a 4" opening along the length of one star point. Clip the points and curves if necessary, and turn the pillow right side out.

4"

6. Insert small pieces of stuffing through the opening, using a chopstick or other tool with a blunt end to stuff the star points. Whipstitch the opening closed, and put a little sparkle in someone's life!

∾◎ MAKE IT SIMPLE! ◎∾

For quick gifts or as a child's project, use polar fleece; fuzzy, velour-textured fabric such as Minkee; or wool to make your pillow. Hand stitch the edges with perle cotton, yarn, or embroidery floss, or machine stitch with either a decorative or straight stitch on top. It's so easy, you can conjure up an entire galaxy in an afternoon!

Star pillow pattern

Enlarge 300%.

BE BRAVE QUILT

Inspiration comes in many colors and small details. Tucked among the leaves and vines of this quilt are daily affirmations to fortify, inspire, and empower us for the days ahead. Choose as many or as few of the affirmations as you like for your quilt, or make up your own. Using a wide variety of fabrics contributes to the warm, scrappy personality of this quilt, so be sure to check your scrap basket . . . and your friends' scraps, too!
—Anne and Linda

MATERIALS

Yardage is based on 42"-wide fabric unless otherwise noted.

2½ yards (total) of a wide assortment of fabrics for pieced bars

1⅝ yards of light tone-on-tone print for appliqué background

½ yard of dark fabric for border

¼ yard *each* of 7 assorted fabrics for solid bars

6 fat eighths of assorted green fabrics for leaves

5 yards of fabric for backing

¾ yard of green fabric for binding

61" x 89" piece of batting

10 yards of ⅜"-wide grosgrain ribbon for vines*

1 yard of fusible web

Permanent fabric-marking pens for affirmations (optional)

See "Curving Ribbon" on page 67 for suggestions.

CUTTING

Cut all strips from the crosswise grain unless otherwise noted.

From *each* ¼ yard of assorted fabric, cut:
◆ 2 strips, 2" x 40" (14 total)

From the 2½ yards of assorted fabric, cut *a total of*:
◆ 40 strips, 2" x 40"

From the *lengthwise grain* of the light tone-on-tone print, cut:
◆ 6 strips, 5" x 54"

From the dark fabric, cut:
◆ 7 strips, 2" x 40"

From the green fabric for binding, cut:
◆ 8 strips, 2½" x 40"

MAKING THE BARS

1. Using the strips cut from the ¼-yard pieces, stitch two matching 2" x 40" strips together end to end; press. Make seven strips. Trim each strip to 2" x 54".

2. Stitch the 2" x 40" strips of assorted fabric together end to end to make a series of long (175" to 225") strips that total approximately 1600". From these long strips, trim a total of

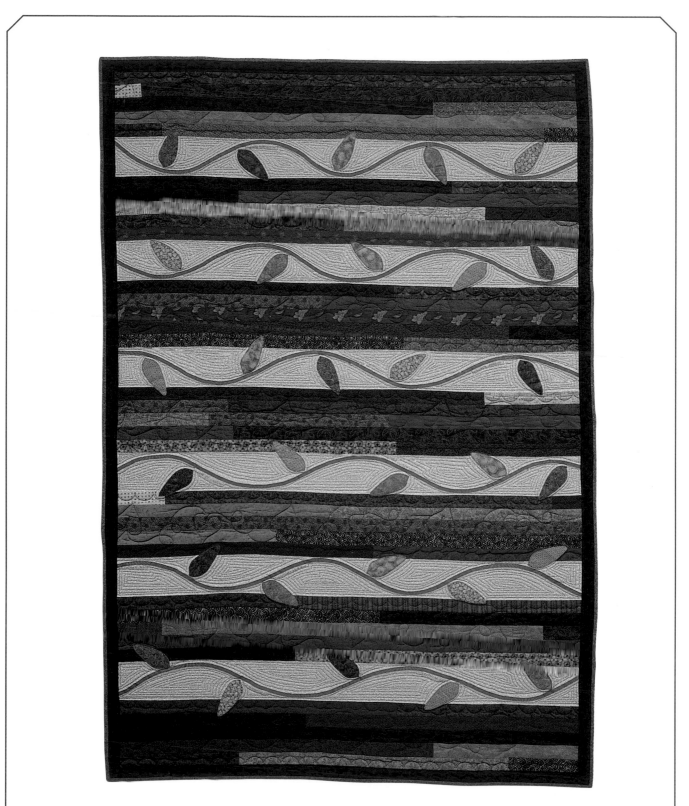

Be Brave Quilt

By Anne Moscicki and Linda Wyckoff-Hickey, 55" x 83".

Quilted by Celeste Marshall.

28 strips, 2" x 54", making sure there is no seam within 3" of either end of any strip. If necessary, you can use the trimmings to complete the required number of 54"-long strips.

3. Lay out the solid and pieced bars and the 5" x 54" background strips to make six rows as shown, arranging the colors and prints in a way that pleases you. Sew the bars and strips together to complete each row. Add each successive strip from the opposite end to reduce bowing in the finished row. Press the seam allowances open. Do not sew the rows together yet; you will appliqué and trim them first.

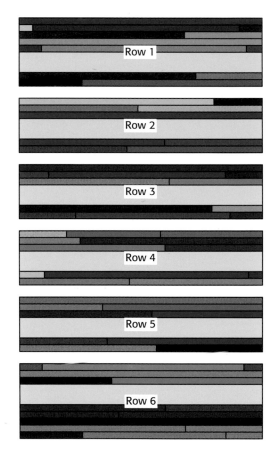

APPLIQUÉING THE LEAVES AND VINES

We allowed the vines in the pictured quilt to ramble gently and randomly along each background strip. You may prefer to place them evenly. In either case, refer to "All Tied Up! Working with Ribbon" on page 67 for guidance as needed.

1. Referring to the quilt photo on page 63, arrange the ribbon on one background strip, shaping it gently and pinning it securely into place; trim. Press the pinned vine with a steam iron. Machine stitch both edges of the vine using a straight stitch or other stitch that will firmly anchor the ribbon in place. Refer to "Tips and Techniques for Decorative Stitching" on page 50 for ideas. Repeat for all six background strips.

2. Use the pattern on page 66 and paper or template material to make a leaf template. Trace 30 leaves onto the paper side of the fusible web, leaving approximately ½" between the shapes. Cut out the leaves about ¼" beyond the traced lines. Press five leaves, paper side up, onto the wrong side of one green leaf fabric, using heat and pressure according to the manufacturer's instructions. Cut out the leaves on the traced line. Repeat using the remaining fusible-web shapes and leaf fabrics to make a total of 30 leaves.

3. Place five assorted leaves along the vine on each background strip, varying the angles of the leaves and allowing some to overlap onto the pieced bars. (You will trim the rows slightly after you complete the appliqué, so do not place any leaves within 3" of either end of the row.) Fuse and stitch the leaves into place using a blanket stitch or other decorative stitch; refer to "Tips and Techniques for Decorative Stitching" on page 50 for ideas.

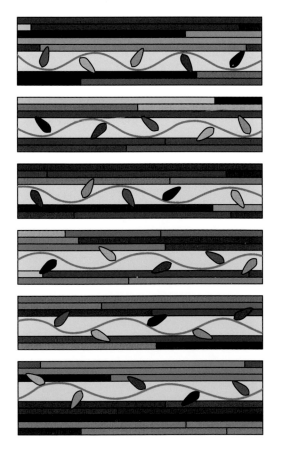

ASSEMBLING THE QUILT

1. Trim each appliquéd row to 52" long.

2. Stitch the rows together, pressing the seam allowances open.

3. Refer to "Adding a Straight Border" on page 106 as needed to measure, join and/or trim, and sew the 2"-wide dark border to the quilt.

ADDING THE AFFIRMATIONS

Write each affirmation you plan to add to the quilt on a small scrap of paper. Pin them to the quilt, balancing their placement along the vine rows.

Remove the paper scraps one by one and write the affirmations onto the quilt. If you wish, you can write the words first with a removable fabric marker. When you are pleased with the look and placement, write over the words with a permanent fabric marker to make them permanent.

FINISHING THE QUILT

1. Refer to "Quilting Basics" on page 104 as needed to finish your quilt. Prepare the quilt backing, and then layer and baste together the backing, batting, and quilt top.

2. Quilt as desired. In the pictured quilt, leafy vines adorn the barred rows, and concentric outline quilting defines the appliquéd leaves and vines.

3. Trim the excess batting and backing fabric, remove the basting, and use the 2½"-wide strips to bind your quilt.

4. Add a hanging sleeve, label, or pocket to your quilt, if desired. Refer to "Finishing Touches" on page 109 for methods, tips, and ideas.

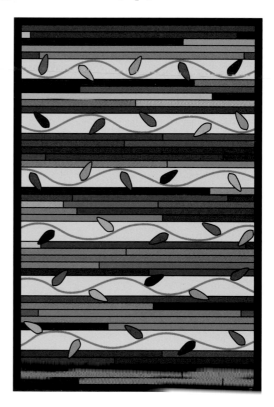

❧ MAKE IT UNIQUE! ❧

Whether you meditate, pray, or hold a loved one in your thoughts, the words from your heart become tangible encouragement in this special quilt. The words that appear on our quilt are listed below, but only to start you off! Think about passages from books, songs, hymns, poems, sonnets, or other meaningful words to share your hopes.

If you're uncomfortable applying permanent ink to your quilt, warm up on paper. You may also ask a friend with lovely handwriting or calligraphy skills to help out, but don't discount the sentimental value of penning your words in your own distinct hand. Don't you feel the pang of recognition when you come across one of your grandmother's handwritten recipes? Allow the ones who love you to feel that same sweet recall someday in the future!

Our affirmations:

be brave ◆ breathe deeply ◆ celebrate daily ◆ count blessings ◆ live abundantly ◆ keep promises

honor family ◆ love truly ◆ cherish freedom ◆ grow strong ◆ spread joy ◆ cultivate peace ◆ live generously

Leaf
Cut 30.

Pattern is reversed for fusible appliqué.
No seam allowance is included.

All Tied Up!
Working with Ribbon

Ribbon can be both a timesaving and eye-catching addition to your quilts. Its functional finished edges make it a great choice for handles, casings for drawstrings, binding, and edging. The range of distinctive textures, patterns, and colors add a unique touch to your finished project. Keep a few tips in mind, and then enjoy adding this new dimension to your embellishments!

- Choose the right ribbon for your project by considering the ribbon's weight and flexibility in addition to its color. There are thousands of different weaves, finishes, and fibers to choose from, so experiment to find one that is perfect for your project.

- Check manufacturer's instructions on fiber content and cleaning care before securing ribbon permanently to your project.

- If you haven't treated yourself to new pins or a fresh sewing-machine needle in a while, this is a good time for a little splurge: dull points can catch delicate fibers and create snags.

MITERED CORNERS

Ribbon works beautifully when appliquéd to serve as an accent on a pieced area, or as a "faux" inner border, as shown in our Baby Love Quilt on page 40. It's easy to create neat, right-angled corners with ribbon.

1. Align the ribbon edge along a marked line or pieced seam. Pin securely. When the ribbon reaches the point where it needs to turn, fold it back along its length.

2. Twist the top of the ribbon to form a neat, right-angled pleat at the corner. Pin securely, and then continue pinning the ribbon into place on the adjacent side. Miter each corner in the same manner, and fold the aligned ribbon ends under for a finished look.

3. Stitch the ribbon along both edges to anchor it to your project. Make a short seam to secure the mitered corner fold, or tack by hand.

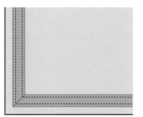

CURVING RIBBON

The distinctive ribbing on grosgrain ribbon helps it form the gentle, rolling curves of the vines in our Be Brave Quilt on page 61. Some grosgrain ribbon has more flexibility than others, depending on how the edges are finished. Look for edges that show the grosgrain's inherent ribbing rather than a solid or flat edge. If you prefer a different ribbon for your curves, test a small portion to make sure that it lies smoothly without puckering or bunching. Different widths, weights, and fiber contents of ribbon react differently to curving. The narrowest, most lightweight ribbon with the highest cotton/natural fiber content allows for a deeper, more precise curve than a wide, heavy synthetic ribbon.

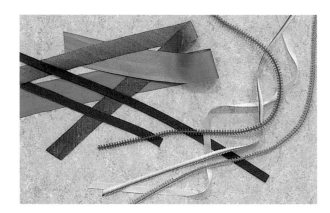

Ribbons for curves and for straight lines

RANDOM CURVES

Whether wildly rambling or gently wandering, random curves add a casual, creative style to your project. If your goal is that natural look, use the same pinning methods shown in the discussion of precise curves that follows, but don't mark your fabric before laying out the ribbon. Leave ½" from the top and bottom edges of the background for seam allowances.

Another method to consider for creating randomly curving vines is the use of bias strips with fusible-web tape, as shown in our Be Just a Little Brave Quilt on page 73; refer to "Adding the Appliqués" on pages 74–75.

PRECISE CURVES

Precise curves re-create the deliberate, manicured look of a formal garden or classic architectural detailing. Repeat them symmetrically in borders or to frame a pieced design.

1. To make even curves, mark the background fabric in halves, thirds, or further increments as desired; the diagrams that follow show a fabric panel marked in quarters. Lay out the highest and lowest points of the curve to meet these marks. Leave ½" from the top and bottom edges of the background for seam allowance. Anchor the high and low points

of the curves in place with pins. Stand back occasionally to view the pinned curves, preferably viewing them on a design wall or other flat surface that gives you a good perspective. Adjust the curves as necessary. If you point all the pins in the same direction, you can remove them easily as you stitch the ribbon edges. This also allows you to press with your steam iron more easily.

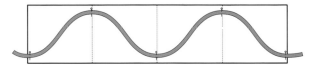

2. Continue adding pins, spacing them farther apart along the straighter parts of the vines and clustering them more heavily on the curves. Use a steam iron as needed to help flatten the ribbon into place.

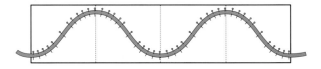

3. Stitch the edges of the ribbon, beginning and ending on the same side of the background piece to reduce puckering. Trim the ribbon and thread ends even with the fabric.

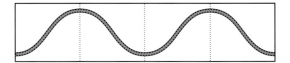

Tranquility Table Runner
or Wall Quilt

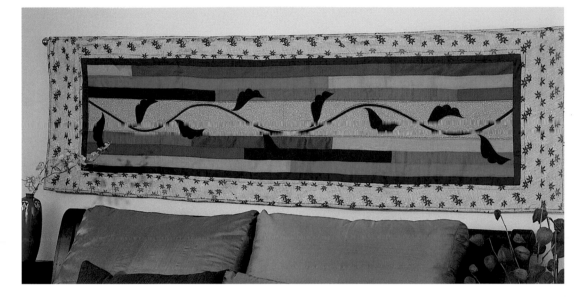

*Sometimes we all need something spectacularly out of the ordinary:
one bite of really deep, dark chocolate, a spritz of exotic perfume,
an extra hour of sleep . . . So treat yourself to a little extra time
searching out fabrics with radiant color and shimmering
textures to bring this elegant project to life!*

—Anne and Linda

MATERIALS

Yardage is based on 42"-wide fabric unless otherwise noted. Be aware that specialty fabrics may come in a variety of widths.

1⅛ yards of fabric for outer border and binding

⅜ yard of light fabric for center panel

¼ yard of fabric for inner border

Assorted 2"-wide fabric strips in a variety of lengths, totaling 400", for pieced bars

2⅝ yards of fabric for backing

27" x 82" piece of batting

¼ yard of 36"-wide faux suede for appliquéd leaves and vines (optional)

½ yard of fusible web (optional)

~ MAKE IT UNIQUE! ~

Whether you choose serene tonal fabrics or glorious brights, try searching outside the usual quilter's stash when looking for materials for this project. Antique textiles, decorator fabrics, luscious silks, swatches rescued from vintage clothing, or an old bag of dressmaker's remnants can provide just the right shimmer, texture, or hue to make the difference between "everyday" and "extraordinary."

- *If you choose fabrics with delicate fibers, be sure your needles and pins are sharp to avoid catching and pulling.*

- *Silks and other fiber combinations may be candidates for excessive fraying. Handle fabric carefully to minimize pulling or stretching, and consider using a serger or running a zigzag stitch along cut edges. We have had our best success laying this project out on a floor or other smooth, flat workspace, rather than putting it up on a design wall that may cling to fraying edges.*

- *As you assemble fabrics, consider which cleaning method—machine washing, hand washing, or dry cleaning—will accommodate the whole variety. Test fabric swatches before you start stitching.*

CUTTING

Cut all strips from the crosswise grain.

From the light fabric, cut:

- ◆ 2 strips, 5" x 40"

From the inner-border fabric, cut:

- ◆ 4 strips, 1½" x 40"

From the outer-border and binding fabric, cut:

- ◆ 4 strips, 3" x 42"
- ◆ 1 strip, 6" x 40"
- ◆ 6 strips, 2½" x 40"

ASSEMBLING THE TABLE RUNNER OR WALL QUILT

1. Stitch the two 5" x 40" light strips together end to end; press. Trim to 5" x 63". Play with the arrangement of the assorted 2"-wide strips to form three bars above and three bars below the center panel, trimming as desired to balance color and stagger seams.

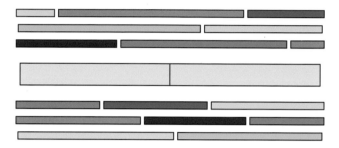

2. Stitch the first row of 2"-wide strips together end to end to form a pieced bar; press. Trim to 63" if necessary. Repeat to stitch all six pieced bars. Join three bars to form a three-bar unit. Make two. Stitch one to the top and one to the bottom of the center panel. Trim the ends to straighten them, as necessary.

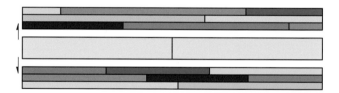

3. The two versions of the project shown on page 71 use different methods for creating the images of leaves and vines. In the silk table runner, the leaves and vines were quilted rather than appliquéd for subtle, elegant results. The bright wall quilt features appliqué. If desired, refer to "Appliquéing the Leaves and Vines" on page 64. Use the patterns on page 72, the faux suede, and the fusible web to appliqué a vine and nine leaves to the center of the table runner or quilt as shown in the photo on page 71.

4. Refer to "Adding a Straight Border" on page 106 as needed to measure, join and/or trim, and sew the 1½"-wide inner-border strips to the sides, top, and bottom of the project. Repeat to sew the 3"-wide outer-border strips to the long sides of the project, and the 6"-wide outer-border strips to the short sides.

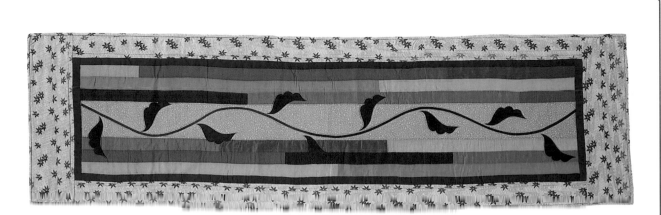

Tranquility Wall Quilt

By Anne Moscicki and Linda Wyckoff-Hickey, 76" x 21".

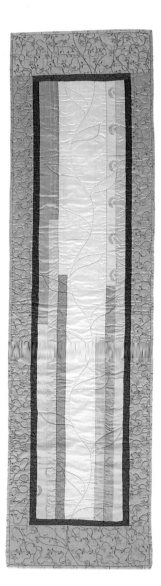

Tranquility Table Runner

By Anne Moscicki and Linda Wyckoff-Hickey,
21" x 76". Quilted by Amy Helmkamp.

FINISHING THE TABLE RUNNER OR WALL QUILT

1. Refer to "Quilting Basics" on page 104 as needed to finish your table runner or quilt. You will not need to piece the backing. Layer and baste together the backing, batting, and quilt top.

2. Quilt as desired. The bright variation shown on page 71 is quilted just outside the inner border, and the appliquéd leaf-and-vine motif is outline quilted.

3. Trim the excess batting and backing fabric, remove the basting, and use the 2½"-wide strips to bind your table runner or quilt.

4. Add a label to your table runner or a hanging sleeve, label, or pocket to your quilt, if desired. Refer to "Finishing Touches" on page 109 for methods, tips, and ideas.

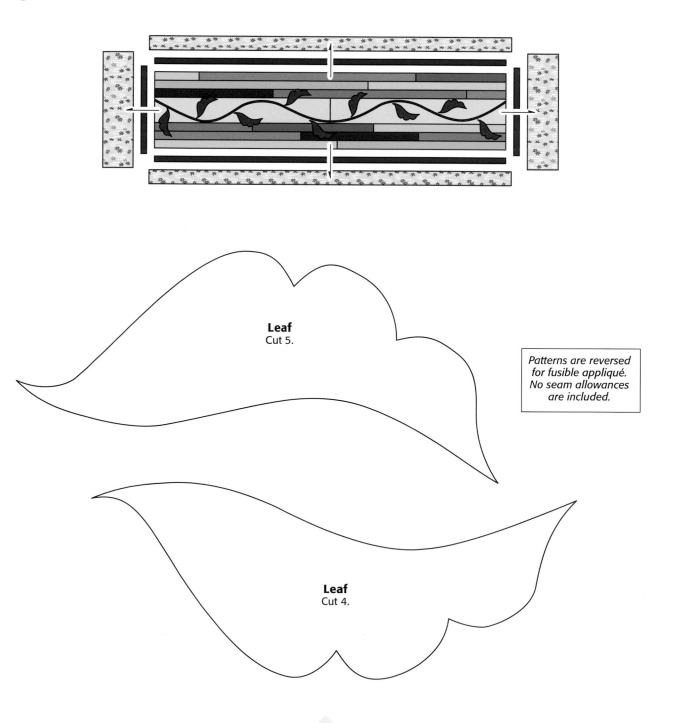

Leaf
Cut 5.

*Patterns are reversed
for fusible appliqué.
No seam allowances
are included.*

Leaf
Cut 4.

BE JUST
A LITTLE BRAVE QUILT

Rescaling the proportions of the Be Brave Quilt and using sweet, classic floral prints results in an easy and delightful small quilt or wall hanging. Try the freeform curly vines made from bias strips as shown here; create designs with ribbon, referring to "All Tied Up! Working with Ribbon" on page 67; or use your favorite method of appliqué.

MATERIALS

Yardage is based on 42"-wide fabric.

1⅝ yards of floral fabric for outer border and binding

¾ yard of green fabric for bias-cut appliquéd vines

⅝ yard of light fabric for appliqué background

⅜ yard *each* of 5 coordinating prints for pieced rows

⅜ yard of fabric for inner border

Assorted green scraps for appliquéd leaves

3⅝ yards of fabric for backing

58" x 64" piece of batting

¼"-wide fusible tape

½ yard of fusible web

CUTTING

Cut all strips from the crosswise grain.

From *each* of the 5 coordinating prints, cut:

◆ 6 strips, 1½" x 40" (30 total)*

From the light fabric, cut:

◆ 5 strips, 3½" x 40"*

From the green fabric for vines, cut:

◆ ⅜" x 20" (minimum) bias strips to total 300"

From the inner-border fabric, cut:

◆ 5 strips, 1½" x 40"

From the outer-border and binding fabric, cut:

◆ 6 strips, 6" x 40"

◆ 6 strips, 2½" x 40"

*Be sure to remove selvage from these strips.

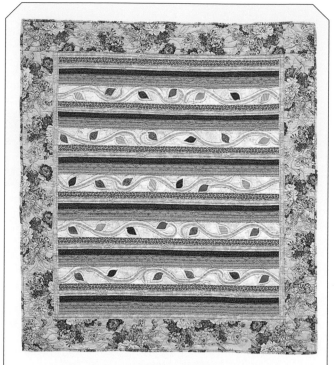

Be Just a Little Brave Quilt

By Anne Moscicki and Linda Wyckoff-Hickey,
52" x 58". Quilted by Linda Humfeld.

MAKING THE PIECED ROWS

Sew one 1½"-wide strip of each coordinating print together along the long edges to make a strip set as shown. Alternate the direction of the seam as you add each new strip. Press the seams open. Make six identical strip sets.

Make 6.

ADDING THE APPLIQUÉS

Just like the morning glories that volunteer along the fence outside our studio window, these vines ramble gently and randomly across this charming quilt. Enjoy their meanderings, and don't worry about precision placement!

If you haven't tried this freehand method of placing vines, play with scraps first to get the feel for how the vines twist and turn. You may choose to mark the vine placement lightly prior to pressing the vines into place, but do at least try making them freehand. Then relax and have fun as you create a garden of leafy vines for your quilt! (Of course, you may substitute any other method that you prefer for making and appliquéing the vines.)

Note that the vines will extend past the side edges of the background strips, and should be placed at least ⅜" from the top and bottom edges to allow for seams. Mark the background with the seam allowance if desired.

1. Follow the manufacturer's directions to apply a strip of fusible tape to the back of each ⅜"-wide bias strip. Remove the paper backing.

2. Referring to the diagram at right for placement suggestions, use a hot iron to anchor a bias strip at one end of a 3½"-wide background strip. With the bias strip in your left hand (if you are right-handed; reverse if you are left-handed!) and the iron in your right, iron the vine into place in one motion. Keep your left hand about 8" ahead of the iron tip and maneuver the vine into place by gently pulling it against the weight of the iron. The heat will anchor it as you go. Trim the end of the vine at a 45° angle to finish. Repeat to place vines on the four remaining background strips.

3. Secure the vine edges with a hand or machine straight stitch, blanket stitch, or other decorative stitch. Refer to "Tips and Techniques for Decorative Stitching" on page 50 as necessary.

4. Use the patterns on page 76 and paper or template material to make leaf templates. Trace 34 leaves (17 of each) onto the paper side of the fusible web, leaving approximately ½" between the shapes. Cut out the leaves about ¼" beyond the traced lines. Press the leaves, paper side up, onto the wrong side of the green leaf fabrics, using heat and pressure according to the manufacturer's instructions. Cut out the leaves on the traced lines.

5. Arrange the leaves along the vines on each light background row. Vary the angles, and feel free to place more or fewer leaves, depending on your preference and the areas created around the vines.

6. Fuse and stitch the leaves into place with a blanket stitch or other decorative stitch. Refer to "Tips and Techniques for Decorative Stitching" on page 50 as necessary.

Assembling the Quilt

1. Refer to the quilt photo on page 74 and the diagram that follows to arrange the pieced and appliquéd rows, alternating them as shown. Sew the rows together. Press the seam allowances open.

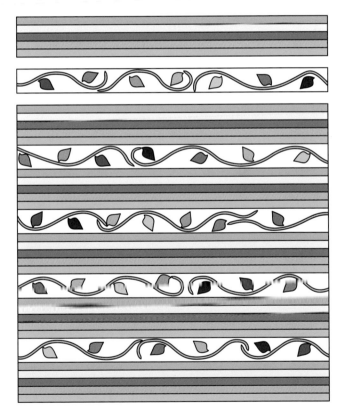

2. Refer to "Adding a Straight Border" on page 106 as needed to measure, join and/or trim, and sew the 1½"-wide inner-border strips and 6"-wide outer-border strips to the quilt.

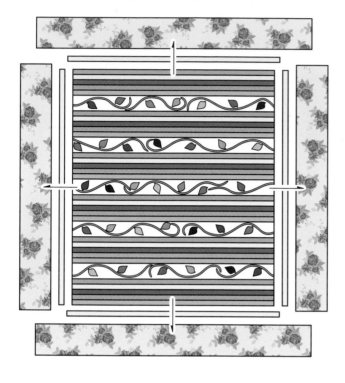

FINISHING THE QUILT

1. Refer to "Quilting Basics" on page 104 as needed to finish your quilt. Prepare the quilt backing, and then layer and baste together the backing, batting, and quilt top.

2. Quilt as desired. In the pictured quilt, the leaves and vines were outlined with the addition of quilted tendrils reaching into the pieced rows. The pieced rows were quilted with an outline echoing the seams, while a feathery floral garland wraps around the border.

3. Trim the excess batting and backing fabric, remove the basting, and use the 2½"-wide strips to bind your quilt.

4. Add a hanging sleeve, label, or pocket to your quilt, if desired. Refer to "Finishing Touches" on page 109 for methods, tips, and ideas.

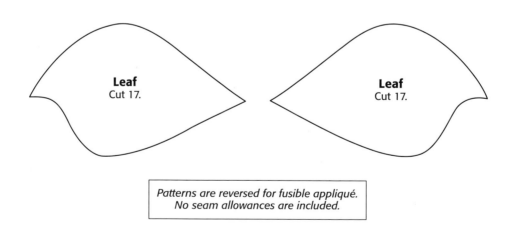

Leaf
Cut 17.

Leaf
Cut 17.

Patterns are reversed for fusible appliqué.
No seam allowances are included.

CHECKERBOARD

Our family looks forward to Oregon's rainy winters, laced with the rare snow day—Hooray! No school! Cancel every plan and chore without guilt! It's time to get out the candles, crafts, and board games as we spend the day with each other and whatever friends brave the elements to join in. With a history dating back 4,000 years to the temples of Thebes, the oldest game in the world is sure to make playful memories for everyone. The simple Checkerboard and Woven Wool Pillows are child's play to create with wool and ribbon accents, plus they make fun additions to any playroom, classroom, or family room. Don't forget to add the most magical ingredient of all: your time to play the game with someone you love!

—Anne

MATERIALS

1 yard of 36"-wide wool for checkerboard background

⅞ yard of 36"-wide light-colored wool for checkerboard squares

⅞ yard of 36"-wide dark-colored wool for checkerboard squares

7 yards of 1½"-wide silk ribbon or other lightweight ribbon for checkerboard accent and binding*

¼"-wide fusible tape

Refer to "All Tied Up! Working with Ribbon" on page 67 for suggestions.

CUTTING

Cut all strips from the crosswise grain.

From *each* piece of light and dark wool, cut:

◆ 8 strips, 3" x 30" (16 total)

From the background wool, cut:

◆ 1 square, 31" x 31"

ASSEMBLING THE CHECKERBOARD

1. Use the pattern on page 82 and paper or template material to make a template for the scallop. Trace the scallop template onto both ends of each 3" x 30" wool strip. Use scissors to trim along the curves of the marked scallops. Make eight scalloped strips of each color (16 total).

Checkerboard
By Anne Moscicki and Linda Wyckoff-Hickey, 31" x 31".

2. Lay out all the strips of one color horizontally on your workspace as shown, butting them together and aligning the ends. Lay out the strips of the other color vertically. Measure and mark the center of each set of strips as shown; this will allow you to align the strips as you weave them.

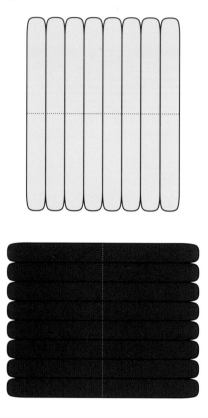

3. Fold back alternating horizontal strips to the center mark as shown. Align one vertical strip with the marks on the horizontal strips, and with its own center mark aligned with the center of the horizontal strips. Pin the vertical strip to the flat horizontal strips to hold it in place. Lay the folded horizontal strips back into place and pin the vertical strip to them.

4. Fold back the alternating set of horizontal strips. Align and tuck the second vertical strip into place, butting the edges as close to the first strip as possible without moving the strips out of alignment. Pin the second vertical strip to the flat set of strips. Lay the folded horizontal strips back into place and pin the second vertical strip to them.

5. Continue to fold alternating horizontal strips, aligning and pinning two more vertical strips into place. The strips should butt firmly against each other, without distorting the wool.

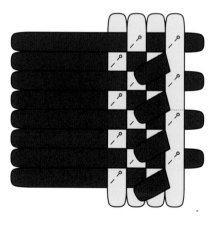

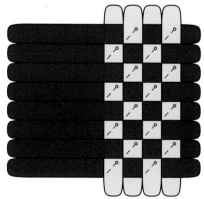

6. When you've finished half of the checkerboard, carefully turn the partially woven piece 180° and weave the other half as shown.

7. Stitch the woven strips together approximately ⅛" from the edges in one continuous line of stitching. Begin at one corner of the scalloped border, just outside the woven strip area as shown, removing pins *only* as necessary to complete the stitching. Complete the row and turn the checkerboard 90° in your machine, stitching into the scalloped border area before turning the checkerboard 90° to stitch the other edge of the row. Continue until all the rows are stitched horizontally.

Begin stitching.

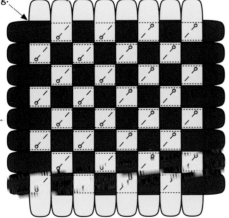

8. Turn the checkerboard and repeat step 7 to stitch the remaining strip edges. Remove all pins.

End stitching.

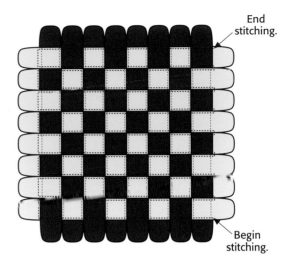

Begin stitching.

9. Center the stitched checkerboard on the 31" background square and pin in place.

10. Fold the two long edges of the ribbon, right side out, to meet in the center, making a ¾"-wide strip as shown; press. Follow the manufacturer's directions to add one strip of fusible tape to each side of the center join as shown. Remove the paper backing.

11. Place and pin the folded ribbon, fusible side down, around the edges of the woven strips, just outside the stitching. Miter the corners of the ribbon; trim the excess. Fuse the ribbon in place, following the web manufacturer's guidelines with respect to the

fabric content of the ribbon. Topstitch both sides of the ribbon about 1⁄16" from the folded edge to hold both the ribbon and the background securely.

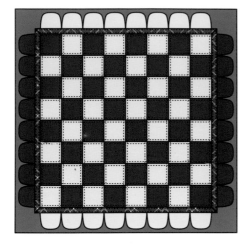

12. Place the checkerboard on your ironing board. Wrap the remaining ribbon snugly around the outside edge of the background square so that equal amounts of ribbon "binding" are visible on both front and back; trim the excess length. Fuse the ribbon into place, folding the corners to create a miter on both front and back. Topstitch 1⁄8" from the inner edge of the ribbon and stitch or tack the mitered fold to secure. Checkers, anyone?

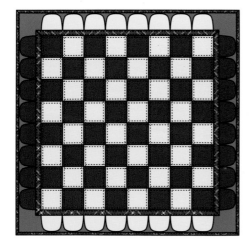

❧ CREATIVE ☙ CHECKER GAME PIECES

Use fun and unusual game pieces to make playtime unforgettable!

- *Foreign coins from travels in the past or planned for the future*

- *A small bough collected during a woodland adventure, cut into disks and painted or marked with permanent pens*

- *Wool scraps cut into shapes to layer with stitches, buttons, or other embellishments*

- *Painted stones*

- *Chocolate kisses wrapped in different-colored foils*

- *Sandwich cookies in various flavors*

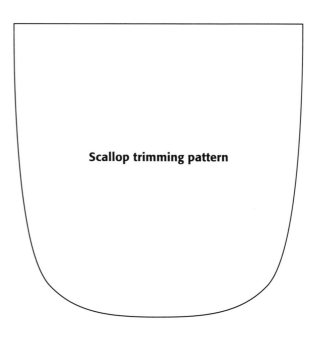

Scallop trimming pattern

WOVEN WOOL PILLOWS

By Anne Moscicki and Linda Wyckoff-Hickey, 21" x 21".

Rustic wool takes on a graphic, modern style in these colorful woven pillows. The simplest of decorative or straight stitches adds texture and a hint of argyle-inspired interest while serving to secure the weaving.

MATERIALS FOR ONE PILLOW

20 strips, 1½" x 18", of wool in a variety of colors for checkerboard

1 square, 21" x 21", of wool for checkerboard background

2 rectangles, 12" x 21", of wool for pillow backing

2 yards of 1½"-wide silk ribbon or other lightweight ribbon for checkerboard binding*

16" square pillow form

¼"-wide fusible tape

*Refer to "All Tied Up! Working with Ribbon" on page 67 for suggestions.

MAKING THE PILLOW

1. Separate the 1½"-wide wool strips into two piles of 10 strips each. Repeat "Assembling the Checkerboard," steps 2–6 on pages 78–81, to weave the two sets of strips into a checkerboard formation as shown. Pin the woven strips securely.

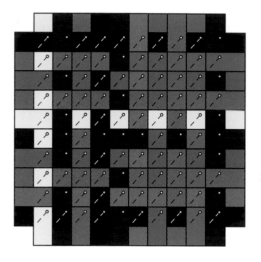

2. Trim the ends of the woven strips, leaving an approximate 1" overhang; this will make it easier to add the stitching.

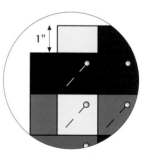

3. Using either a decorative stitch, a straight stitch, or a combination of the two, stitch along one center diagonal of the woven strips, removing the pins as you stitch.

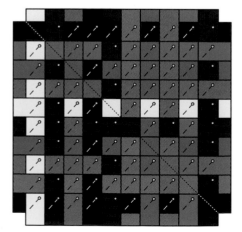

4. Continue stitching diagonal lines in one direction, and then repeat in the opposite direction to create a cross-hatch pattern as shown. Trim as in step 2.

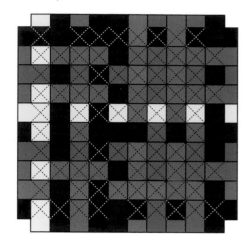

5. Use a straight stitch to outline the edges of the checkerboard as shown, staying as close to the edge as possible. Trim the stitched piece close to the stitching to square the checkerboard and remove the excess strip ends.

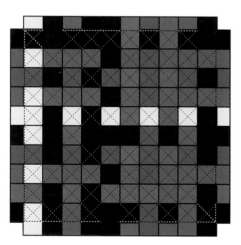

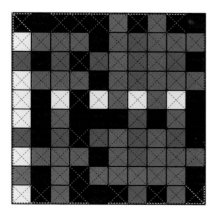

6. Refer to "Assembling the Checkerboard," step 10 on page 81, to prepare the ribbon for fusing.

7. Place the checkerboard on your ironing board. Wrap the ribbon snugly around the outside edge of the checkerboard so that equal amounts of ribbon "binding" are visible on both front and back; trim the excess length. Fuse the ribbon into place, folding the corners to create a miter on both front and back.

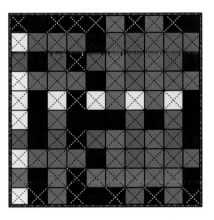

8. Center the bound checkerboard on the 21" background square and pin in place. Topstitch ⅛" from the inner edge of the ribbon to secure the checkerboard to the background.

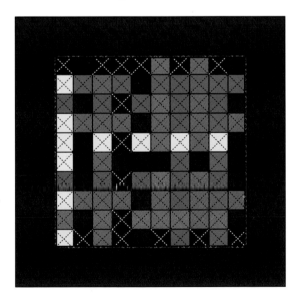

9. Place the pillow top wrong side down on a clean, flat workspace. Position the two backing pieces over the pillow top as shown, aligning the backing edges with the raw edges of the top. (The backing pieces will overlap.) Pin the backing pieces in place.

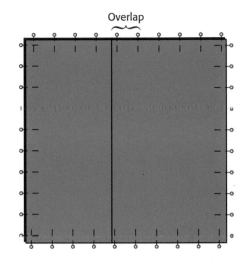

10. Turn the pillow over. Mark and stitch 1" from the edges of the bound checkerboard. Insert the pillow form, and then sit back, relax, and enjoy your handiwork.

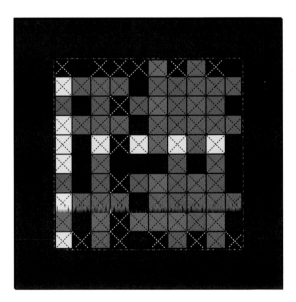

The silver lining that surrounds hard times is often strength of character and a sense of humor. If you've listened to your parents and grandparents reminisce about their lives, chances are you've heard of days when there wasn't a scrap worth wasting. This quilt design honors that hard-learned lesson—as valuable today as it was necessary then—by using two simple "flips" on each block to stretch one project into two.
—*Anne and Linda*

MATERIALS

Yardage is based on 42"-wide fabric.

2½ yards of fabric B

1½ yards of fabric for outer border

1¼ yards of fabric A

⅞ yard of fabric for inner border

¼ yard *each* of 24 assorted fabrics for fabric C*

7½ yards of fabric for backing

¾ yard of fabric for binding

89" x 89" piece of batting

You may substitute 144 squares, 6" x 6", of assorted scraps.

CUTTING

Cut all strips from the crosswise grain.

From fabric B, cut:

◆ 18 strips, 4½" x 42"; subcut into 144 squares, 4½" x 4½"

From *each* fabric C, cut:

◆ 1 strip, 6" x 40"; subcut into 6 squares, 6" x 6" (144 total)*

From fabric A, cut:

◆ 12 strips, 3¼" x 42"; subcut into 144 squares, 3¼" x 3¼"

From the inner-border fabric, cut:

◆ 7 strips, 3½" x 42"

From the outer-border fabric, cut:

◆ 8 strips, 6" x 42"

From the binding fabric, cut:

◆ 9 strips, 2½" x 42"

You will not need to cut these pieces if you are using precut scraps.

MAKING THE DOUBLE BACK-FLIPS BLOCK

You will use one each of fabrics A, B, and C to complete the Double Back-Flips block shown below. This is the block you will use to construct the Scotch Granny Quilt. The method used to construct each block yields two additional blocks that can be used to construct the Scotch Granny Throw shown on page 92.

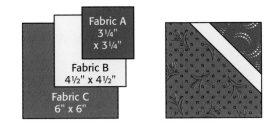

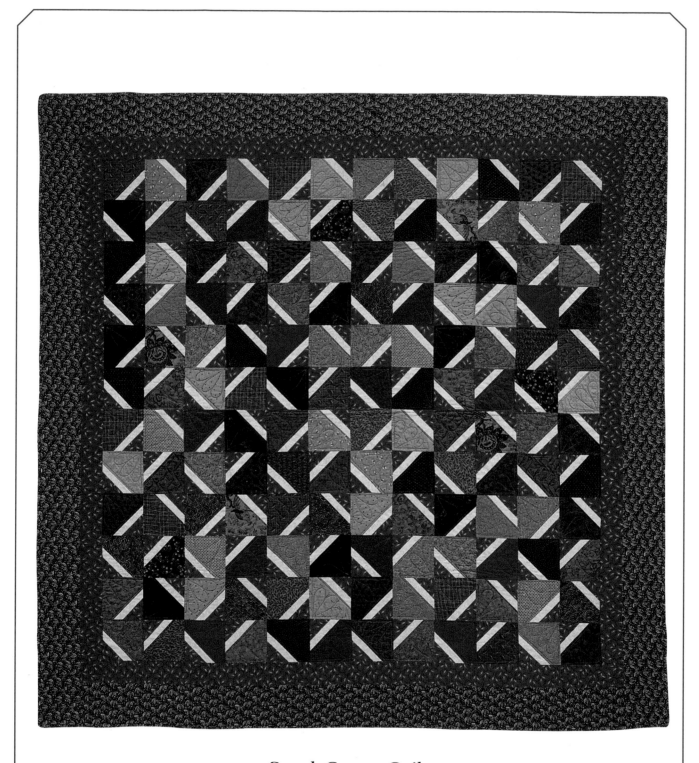

Scotch Granny Quilt

By Anne Moscicki and Linda Wyckoff-Hickey, 83" x 83".

Quilted by Celeste Marshall.

1. Place one fabric B square over the upper-right corner of a fabric C square, right sides together and raw edges aligned. Mark the smaller square once diagonally from corner to corner, and then move the ruler ½" toward the upper-right corner of the square and mark a second line parallel to the first as shown. Sew on both marked lines. Cut the squares halfway between the two stitching lines. Make 144.

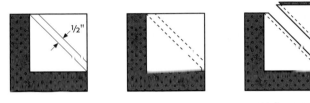

Make 144.

2. Fold out the corners on each unit from step 1; press. Reserve the small half-square-triangle units for the Scotch Granny Throw or another project. Proceed with the remaining steps to finish piecing the Double Back-Flips blocks.

3. Repeat step 1 using the fabric A squares and the larger units from step 2. Make 144.

Make 144.

4. Fold the corners out on each unit from step 3; press. Reserve the small half-square-triangle units for the Scotch Granny Throw or another project. Square each large Double Back-Flips block to 6" x 6" as necessary to complete this quilt.

ASSEMBLING THE QUILT

Refer to the diagram below and the quilt photo on page 88. Lay out the blocks in 12 horizontal rows of 12 blocks each, rotating them as shown and balancing the placement of color as you go. Sew the blocks together into rows; press. Sew the rows together, interlocking the seam allowances; press.

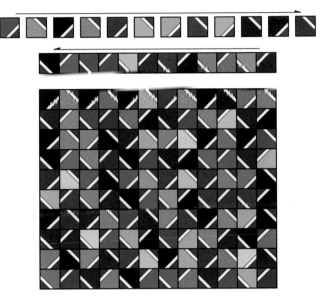

ADDING THE BORDERS

Refer to "Adding a Straight Border" on page 106 as needed to measure, join and/or trim, and sew the 3½"-wide inner-border strips and 6"-wide outer-border strips to the quilt.

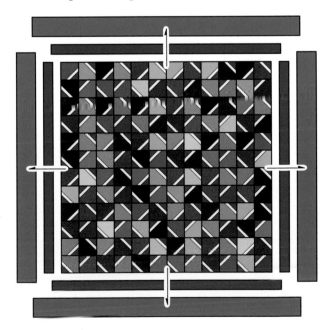

FINISHING THE QUILT

1. Refer to "Quilting Basics" on page 104 as needed to finish your quilt. Prepare the quilt backing, and then layer and baste together the backing, batting, and quilt top.

2. Quilt as desired. In the pictured quilt, each "bow-tie" shape is outline quilted ¼" from the pieced edge. A three-petal fan emerges from the corner of each outline. Thanks to our wonderful quilter, Celeste Marshall, for this lovely quilting design.

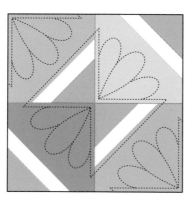

Scotch Granny at the Beach Quilt

By Anne Moscicki and Linda Wyckoff-Hickey, 83" x 83". Quilted by Celeste Marshall. The sparkling quality of bright batiks adds tropical splendor to this version of the Scotch Granny Quilt.

3. Trim the excess batting and backing fabric, remove the basting, and use the 2½"-wide strips to bind your quilt.

4. Add a hanging sleeve, label, or pocket to your quilt, if desired. Refer to "Finishing Touches" on page 109 for methods, tips, and ideas.

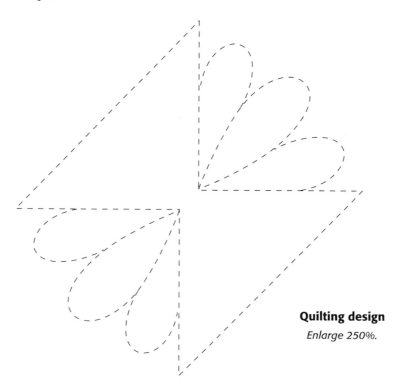

Quilting design
Enlarge 250%.

Using Leftovers to Make the Scotch Granny Throw

Making the Throw

Waste not, want not! What more could you wish for than two quilts for the fabric of one? Now the leftover blocks you've already made during construction of the Scotch Granny Quilt, shown on page 88, are ready to sparkle and shine on their own in this playful throw. On page 94 we've also included yardage, a cutting list, and instructions if you just want to make the throw "from scratch."

Materials

Yardage is based on 42"-wide fabric.

⅝ yard of fabric for outer border

⅝ yard of fabric for binding

3⅛ yards of fabric for backing

54" x 54" piece of batting

Scotch Granny Throw

By Anne Moscicki and Linda Wyckoff-Hickey,
48" x 48". Quilted by Celeste Marshall.

CUTTING

Cut all strips from the crosswise grain.

From the outer-border fabric, cut:

- ◆ 5 strips, 3" x 42"

From the binding fabric, cut:

- ◆ 6 strips, 2½" x 42"

ASSEMBLING THE PINWHEEL BLOCKS

You will use the larger half-square-triangle units from the Scotch Granny Quilt to make these blocks. Before you begin, trim the units to 3½" as necessary.

Arrange four half-square-triangle units into two rows of two blocks each as shown, matching colors whenever possible. Part of the scrappy, quirky charm of this quilt is that some of the blocks won't match

up perfectly, so don't worry if you're mixing reds and blues in one pinwheel. Make 36 Pinwheel blocks, squaring each to 6½" as necessary.

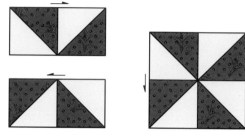

Make 36.

ASSEMBLING THE QUILT CENTER

Refer to the quilt photo at left and the diagram that follows. Lay out the Pinwheel blocks in six horizontal rows of six blocks each as shown, balancing the placement of color as you go. Sew the blocks together into rows; press. Sew the rows together, interlocking the seam allowances; press.

MAKING THE PIECED INNER BORDER

You will use the smaller half-square-triangle units from the Scotch Granny Quilt to make these borders. Before you begin, trim the units to 2½" as necessary.

Arrange and sew the half-square-triangle units as shown to make the pieced inner borders. Each side border unit is made from 18 half-square triangles. Make two; press. The longer top and bottom border units are each made from 20 half-square triangles. Make two; press.

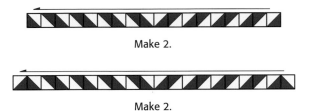

Make 2.

Make 2.

Adding the Borders

1. Refer to "Adding a Straight Border" on page 106 to add the pieced inner-border units to the sides, top, and bottom of the quilt, pinning carefully to match seams. Refer to "Easing In" on page 105 as necessary.

2. Refer to "Adding a Straight Border" again as needed to measure, join and/or trim, and sew the 3"-wide outer-border strips to the quilt.

Finishing the Quilt

1. Refer to "Quilting Basics" on page 104 as needed to finish your quilt. Prepare the quilt backing, and then layer and baste together the backing, batting, and quilt top.

2. Quilt as desired. In the pictured throw, concentric feathered wreaths swirl across the pieced Pinwheel blocks. The geometric piecing of the borders is echoed in the border quilting.

3. Trim the excess batting and backing fabric, remove the basting, and use the 2½"-wide strips to bind your quilt.

4. Add a hanging sleeve, label, or pocket to your quilt, if desired. Refer to "Finishing Touches" on page 109 for methods, tips, and ideas.

**Scotch Granny
at the Beach Throw**

*By Anne Moscicki and Linda Wyckoff-Hickey,
48½" x 48½". Quilted by Celeste Marshall.
Exuberant colors enhance the playful shapes
of this Scotch Granny Throw—sure to
add a bright spot to anyone's day.*

Making the Scotch Granny Throw from Scratch

If you don't have leftover blocks from making the Scotch Granny Quilt (page 86), follow these directions to make the Scotch Granny Throw from scratch.

MATERIALS

Yardage is based on 42"-wide fabric. Yardages for the outer border, binding, backing, and batting are identical to those listed on page 91 for the Scotch Granny Throw. In addition, you will need:

1½ yards of fabric A

⅜ yard of fabric C

¼ yard *each* of 12 assorted fabrics for fabric B*

You may substitute 72 squares, 4⅜" x 4⅜", of assorted scraps.

CUTTING

Cut all strips from the crosswise grain.

Note: Follow the cutting instructions for the outer border and binding listed on page 92 for the Scotch Granny Throw. In addition, you will need to cut:

From fabric A:

◆ 9 strips, 4⅜" x 40"; subcut into 72 squares, 4⅜" x 4⅜"

◆ 3 strips, 2⅞" x 40"; subcut into 38 squares, 2⅞" x 2⅞"

From *each* fabric B:

◆ 1 strip, 4⅜" x 40"; subcut into 6 squares, 4⅜" x 4⅜" (72 total)*

From fabric C:

◆ 3 strips, 2⅞" x 40"; subcut into 38 squares, 2⅞" x 2⅞"

You will not need to cut these pieces if you are using precut scraps.

MAKING THE HALF-SQUARE-TRIANGLE UNITS

1. Layer one 4⅜" fabric A square with one 4⅜" fabric B square, right sides together and raw edges aligned. Mark the top square once diagonally from corner to corner. Make 72. Sew ¼" from the marked line on both sides. Cut on the marked line. Fold open and press the seam allowances toward the lighter fabric to make 144 large half-square triangles.

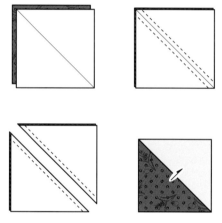

Make 144.

2. Repeat step 1 using the 2⅞" squares of fabric A and fabric C to make 76 small half-square triangles.

COMPLETING THE QUILT

Follow the instructions for assembling the Scotch Granny Throw, beginning with "Assembling the Pinwheel Blocks" on page 92. Use the large half-square-triangle units to make the blocks and the small half-square-triangle units to make the pieced border.

While my mother was being treated for cancer, she found her energy sapped by treatments. A hummingbird feeder outside her window gave her a glimpse into a world of joyous energy, releasing her thoughts to places she could no longer visit in person. Inspired by these tiny winged wonders, the blocks in this cheerful quilt dip and spin.
—Linda

MATERIALS

Yardage is based on 42"-wide fabric. We chose the same fabric for the hummingbird wings and the inner border.

Coordinate two sets of fabrics as follows for the blocks:

Group A Fabrics

⅝ yard for large star points

⅜ yard for center square

⅜ yard for center-square accents

Group B Fabrics

⅝ yard for large star points

⅜ yard for center square

⅜ yard for center-square accents

In addition, you'll need:

2¼ yards of fabric for background

1⅝ yards of fabric for outer border and binding

⅝ yard of fabric for star-point accents

⅝ yard of fabric for inner border

¼ yard of fabric for hummingbird wings

4⅜ yards of fabric for backing

66" x 78" piece of batting

The block corners form the hummingbird wings.

CUTTING

Cut all strips from the crosswise grain.

From *each* center-square accent fabric (groups A and B), cut:

◆ 3 strips, 2½" x 40"; subcut into 40 squares, 2½" x 2½" (80 total)

From *each* center-square fabric (groups A and B), cut:

◆ 2 strips, 4½" x 40"; subcut into 10 squares, 4½" x 4½" (20 total)

From *each* large star-point fabric (groups A and B), cut:

◆ 3 strips, 4⅞" x 40"; subcut into 20 squares, 4⅞" x 4⅞" (40 total)

From the background fabric, cut:

◆ 10 strips, 4½" x 40"; subcut into 80 squares, 4½" x 4½"

◆ 5 strips, 4⅞" x 40"; subcut into 40 squares, 4⅞" x 4⅞"

(continued on page 98)

Hummingbirds Quilt
By Anne Moscicki and Linda Wyckoff-Hickey, 60" x 72".
Quilted by Amy Helmkamp.

From the star-point accent fabric, cut:

- 6 strips, 2½" x 40"; subcut into 80 squares, 2½" x 2½"

From the hummingbird-wing fabric, cut:

- 2 strips, 2½" x 40"; subcut into 24 squares, 2½" x 2½"

From the inner-border fabric, cut:

- 6 strips, 2½" x 40"

From the outer-border and binding fabric, cut:

- 7 strips, 4½" x 40"
- 7 strips, 2½" x 40"

MAKING THE CENTER-SQUARE UNITS

1. Working with fabrics from group A, place one 2½" center-square accent piece over one corner of a 4½" center-square piece, right sides together and raw edges aligned. Mark the small square once diagonally from corner to corner. Sew on the marked line. Trim the seam, leaving a ¼"-wide seam allowance. Fold the corner out; press.

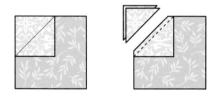

2. Repeat step 1 to stitch a 2½" corner-square accent piece to the corner diagonally opposite the existing accent piece as shown.

3. Stitch a 2½" corner-square accent piece to the remaining corners of each unit from step 2 as shown. Make 10 and label them center square A units.

Center square A units.
Make 10.

4. Use the group B fabrics and repeat steps 1–3 to make 10 center square B units as shown.

Center square B units.
Make 10.

MAKING THE STAR-POINT UNITS

1. Working with fabrics from group A, place one 4⅞" large star-point square with one 4⅞" background square, right sides together and raw edges aligned. Mark the top square once diagonally from corner to corner. Make 20. Sew ¼" from the marked line on both sides. Cut on the marked line. Fold open and press the seam allowances toward the lighter fabric to make 40 group A half-square triangles.

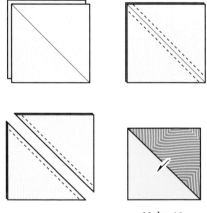

Make 40.

2. Repeat step 1 using the 4⅞" large star-point squares from group B and the remaining 4⅞" background squares to make 40 group B half-square triangles.

Make 40.

3. Place one 2½" star-point accent square over one corner of a unit from step 1, taking care to orient the pieces as shown. Mark the small square once diagonally from corner to corner. Sew on the marked line. Trim the seam, leaving a ¼"-wide seam allowance. Fold the corner out; press. Make 40.

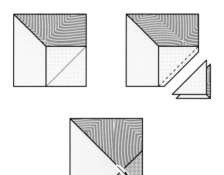

Make 40.

4. Repeat step 3 using the remaining 2½" star-point accent squares and the units from step 2 as shown. Make 40.

Make 40.

Making the Hummingbird-Wing Units

Stitch one 2½" square of hummingbird-wing fabric to a 4½" background square, following the method described in step 1 of "Making the Center-Square Units" on page 98. Make 24.

Make 24.

Assembling the Blocks

Arrange the center-square units, star-point units, hummingbird-wing units, and the remaining 4½" background squares to make the four configurations shown below. Sew the units and squares together into rows; press. Sew the rows together; press. Repeat to make the quantity shown for each configuration.

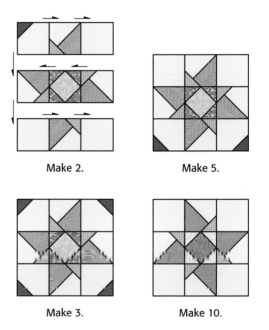

Make 2.   Make 5.

Make 3.   Make 10.

Assembling the Quilt

Refer to the diagram on page 100 to arrange the blocks in five horizontal rows of four blocks each. Take care to orient the blocks exactly as shown. Sew the blocks into rows; press. Sew the rows together, carefully interlocking and pinning the seam allowances to ensure matching corners and neat star points; press.

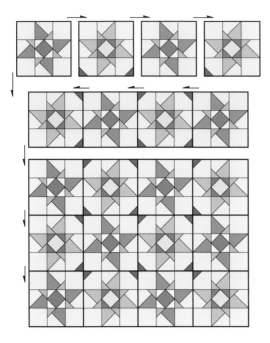

ADDING THE BORDERS

Refer to "Adding a Straight Border" on page 106 as needed to measure, join and/or trim, and sew the 2½"-wide inner-border strips and 4½"-wide outer-border strips to the quilt.

FINISHING THE QUILT

1. Refer to "Quilting Basics" on page 104 as needed to finish your quilt. Prepare the quilt backing, and then layer and baste together the backing, batting, and quilt top.

2. Quilt as desired. In the pictured quilt, the hummingbirds are encircled in a rounded shape that echoes and softens their angles. Swirls and curlicues fill the background. Wavy freehand star points fill the Star Point blocks, and freehand zigzag stitches and a feathery vine finish the borders.

3. Trim the excess batting and backing fabric, remove the basting, and use the 2½"-wide strips to bind your quilt.

4. Add a hanging sleeve, label, or pocket to your quilt, if desired. Refer to "Finishing Touches" on page 109 for methods, tips, and ideas.

HUMMINGBIRDS KEEPSAKE HOLDER

By Anne Moscicki and Linda Wyckoff-Hickey,
approximately 14½" x 17". Quilted by Amy Humfeld.

This easy keepsake holder is large enough for newspaper clippings, magazine tear sheets, yearbooks, photographs, and more. A quick look through your scraps will yield just about everything you need for a gift to remember!

MATERIALS AND CUTTING

Yardage is based on 42"-wide fabric unless otherwise noted. Cut all strips from the crosswise grain.

Coordinate two sets of fabrics as follows for the blocks:

Group A Fabrics

1 square, 4½" x 4½", for center square

4 squares, 2½" x 2½", for center-square accent

2 squares, 4⅞" x 4⅞", for star points

(continued on page 102)

Group B Fabrics

1 square, 4½" x 4½", for center square

4 squares, 2½" x 2½", for center-square accent

2 squares, 4⅞" x 4⅞", for star points

In addition, you'll need:

8 squares, 2½" x 2½", all of the same fabric for star-point accents

8 squares, 4½" x 4½", and 4 squares, 4⅞" x 4⅞", all of the same fabric for background

3 strips, 2¾" x 40", for border; trim 2 strips to 2¾" x 24½". Cut the remaining strip into 2 strips, 2¾" x 17".

1 piece of fabric, 23" x 34", for backing

2 strips of fabric, 2½" x 40", for binding

23" x 34" piece of batting

2 yards of ¼"-wide ribbon for ties

1 yard of 1¼"-wide grosgrain ribbon for tote lining

MAKING THE BLOCKS

1. Follow the instructions for "Making the Center-Square Units" and "Making the Star-Point Units" on page 98. Make one center-square unit and four star-point units each from the group A and group B fabric pieces.

2. Arrange the group A units from step 1 and four 4½" background squares as shown. Sew the units and squares together into rows; press. Sew the rows together; press. Repeat using the group B units from step 1 and the remaining 4½" background squares.

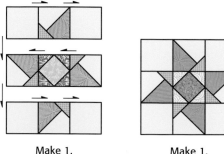

Make 1.   Make 1.

3. Stitch the blocks together side by side as shown. Referring to "Adding a Straight Border" on page 106 as necessary, sew the 2¾" x 24¼" border strips to the top and bottom of the unit; press. Sew the 2¾" x 17" border strips to the sides; press.

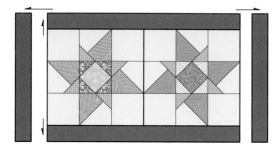

QUILTING

Refer to "Quilting Basics" on page 104 as necessary. Layer the pieced front, batting, and backing fabric; baste. Quilt as desired. Trim the excess batting and backing even with the front.

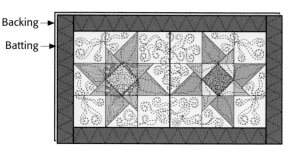

Backing
Batting

ASSEMBLING THE HOLDER

1. Cut the ¼"-wide ribbon into four pieces, 15" long. Pin the ribbons to the opposite short ends of the quilted holder with the ribbons extending toward the center; stitch in place.

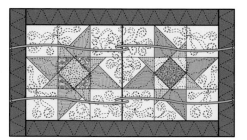

2. Fold the holder in half, wrong side out. Sew the two sides together with a ¼"-wide seam. Cut the 1¼"-wide grosgrain ribbon into two pieces, approximately 14" long. Use the ribbon to cover the seams as shown, tucking the end of the ribbon on the bottom (folded) edge of the holder under for a finished edge. Trim the end of the ribbon on the top edge even with the raw edge of the holder.

Sew sides.

Cover side seams
with grosgrain ribbon.

3. Refer to page 108 of "Quilting Basics" as necessary to prepare the 2½"-wide strips for binding. You will not need to piece the strips. Turn the holder right side out and stitch the binding to the top edge (and over the ends of the ribbon ties). Fold the binding to the wrong side of the holder and whipstitch it into place.

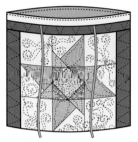

Stitch binding
around top edge.

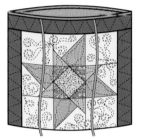

Turn binding to inside of holder
and whipstitch.

⚜ MAKE IT SIMPLE! ⚜

To make this keepsake holder a super-speedy project, omit the pieced block. Choose two ⅝-yard pieces of fabric in addition to the batting, binding, and ribbon called for in "Materials and Cutting" on page 101. Trim each ⅝-yard piece of fabric to 17" x 25", and then complete the layering, quilting, and basting steps described in the project instructions.

For an even easier project, choose a heavyweight fabric, such as wool, faux suede, decorator fabric, or a usable portion of a worn-out quilt, and skip the quilting completely!

Quilting Basics

The most important thing about quilting basics is remembering that they are not the same for every person or even every project. For every tip that works for us, we probably learned different methods from at least three other accomplished quilters! In fact, we often come at a project from differing levels of skill and personal preference. (Linda is a powerhouse of construction techniques, while Anne enjoys tiny detailing.) The techniques that follow are those we rely on in our studio. We include them in hopes that you'll find a little gem that works for you.

Your Mind-Set

No one quilts to add stress to her life! Every step, from choosing patterns and fabrics to stitching that last bit of binding, should be enjoyed. Let go, and don't worry about anyone else's version of right and wrong: if your quilting experiences are not satisfying to you, you must step back and rewrite some of the rules that you quilt by, either consciously or unconsciously.

If you find that you are totally stuck in a creative ditch, give yourself permission to just play for a little while. Try out all your decorative stitches, sewing curvy rows just to enjoy the unusual textured shapes. Pick colors that stretch your usual palette and make a single block. This type of play is not "just fooling around"; it's the essence of your creative spirit. Let it out to play!

Washing Your Fabrics

There are several considerations as you decide whether or not to prewash fabrics for your project: intended use, shrinkage, bleeding, and excessive fraying. We follow these general rules of thumb.

Treat the fabric prior to quilting just as you would the finished quilt. For example, a wall hanging may only need shaking out or vacuuming to remove dust, so prewashing the fabric is not necessary. On the other end of the spectrum, a baby quilt will be washed repeatedly, so wash the fabrics prior to quilting just as you would expect to wash the quilt. If you don't wash the fabrics first, but do wash the finished quilt, be prepared for some puckering. Usually it's not drastic, and may even serve to create a more antique look.

If you do choose to prewash your fabric, fraying can be a concern. You may be able to keep fraying to a minimum in one of the following ways. Note, however, that the yardage requirements in this book, and those of most professionally produced patterns, take the effects of fraying into account.

- Clip each of the four corners of the yardage at an angle.
- Trim the fabric edges with pinking shears or a rotary pinking blade.
- Add a basting stitch to the cut edge of each piece of yardage.
- Last but not least, as you prepare to make a group quilt, ask all the contributors to pretreat the fabric they use in the same way.

Piecing Tools & Methods

Even the simplest tools can be a big help when used properly. The following are a couple we wouldn't want to quilt without.

PINNING

Pins are a quilter's basic, helping to keep the fabrics from pulling out of alignment as you sew. Insert pins at an angle to secure both sides of the seam allowance, whether the seams are pressed open or to one side. This ensures that the seams will lie flat in the quilt top, reducing bulk at the corners and making quilting easier.

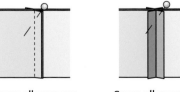

Seam allowances pressed to one side   Seam allowances pressed open

Over time, pins will get dull and snag your fabric. Treat yourself to new ones occasionally, and make sure that the old "snaggy" ones are discarded so they don't get mixed up with the fresh new ones!

SPRAY SIZING

Another lifesaver in our studio is spray sizing. Lighter than starch, it is especially helpful when working with fabrics of differing textures or with bias edges. A light spray of sizing during ironing gives drapey, soft-handed fabrics a bit of "backbone" and will help prevent them from slipping or stretching against other, stiffer fabrics. Flannels are another good candidate for sizing, particularly if you are using a scrappy variety. There is a wide variance among product manufacturers in the weight of their sizing; you want to achieve a cuddly, brushed finish that allows the fabric to stretch as you sew.

MAKING ENDS MEET

Every once in a while, that darn ¼" foot just seems to expand…or shrink! We might blame the differences in block sizes on something as silly as that, but we know the cause is really our own lack of perfection, another humbling reminder that we're only human. And the fact is, we often migrate to our sewing spaces with a lot of life's details on our mind, hoping to stitch out the tensions of the day. Luckily, we are not helpless quilters—we are empowered with three handy techniques to make our blocks fit together as though they were the only important things in our lives: squaring up, short seaming, and easing in.

SQUARING UP

Squaring up is the simplest method of ensuring that blocks will fit together neatly. Start by measuring a wide variety of blocks; are they all at least as large as the pattern instructions call for? If so, just trim the edges as necessary to bring them all to the same size as well as to "true square."

If some of the blocks are larger and some are significantly smaller than you were aiming for, you may make a judgment call to square the blocks to a slightly smaller size. Be aware that doing so may alter the design, as well as the size, of the finished quilt! Depending on the variance of block sizes, you may choose to try the short-seaming or easing-in techniques described in the next sections. Another choice could be to separate the blocks by size and assemble smaller projects: table runners, pillow tops, or baby quilts.

SHORT SEAMING

If, after squaring up the blocks, they still differ in size by ⅛" or less, you can still wind up with a great flat quilt by paying close attention to the short blocks as you assemble the top. Identify all of the "short" blocks by using colored pins as markers.

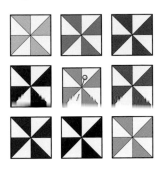

As you sew the blocks into rows, pay special attention to these short blocks, positioning them carefully as you join them to the other blocks. As you place the blocks right sides together to join them, reduce the seam allowance of the short block a bit, but still keep it no less than ⅛". The cut edge of the short block won't meet the edge of its neighbor on the back of your quilt top, but from the front each block will appear as perfect as can be!

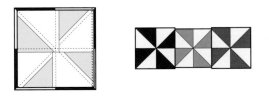

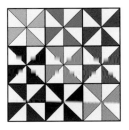

EASING IN

Easing in means making gentle and generous use of your steam iron and pins as you assemble the blocks. Steam or water spray will help the cotton fibers in your pieced top contract or expand slightly to achieve matched corners and points. Your results will vary depending on the individual fabrics used; in the best cases, easing in can make an extremely positive difference in your finished quilt. In general terms, easing in can help in matching seams if you're dealing with a difference of up to ¼" in a 3" to 4" block, depending on the fabrics involved.

To expand a piece to fit, pin the seam allowance on one end into its correct position. Spray the piece lightly with water and pull the piece very gently to expand it. Pin the other end of the piece in its correct position and stretch it gently to fit. Apply the iron gently, a few seconds at a time, until the fabric is thoroughly dry; then stitch.

To fit a piece that is slightly too large, pin both seam allowances into their correct positions. Distribute the excess fabric in half and pin the correct middle of the piece into place. Repeat this "halving" of the excess until you have pins as close as every ¼". Spray the piece lightly with water, and press the iron gently to the edges of the piece to allow the heat to contract the cotton fibers. Continue to apply the iron gently until the fabric is thoroughly dry; then stitch.

Be warned that a quilt pieced with many large ease-ins may not lie perfectly flat in the end. If the blocks vary widely, you might want to consider squaring them to a smaller size.

BORDERS

All the projects featured in this book use one of the following two border techniques.

ADDING A STRAIGHT BORDER

Whether your quilt has one border or several, apply this method to each one for a flat, square finish.

1. Measure the quilt top down the middle, from top to bottom, to find the measurement for the side borders. If necessary, piece the border strips for length, following the steps shown in "Basic Binding Method" on page 108, and trim them to the correct measurement. Stitch the strips to the pieced quilt top on both sides, using easing-in techniques as necessary.

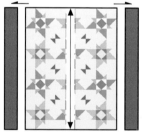

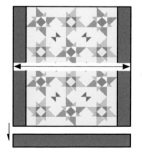

2. Measure the quilt top from side to side, including the borders you've just added, to find the measurement for the top and bottom borders. If necessary, piece the border strips for length, and trim them to the correct measurement. Stitch the strips to the top and bottom of the pieced quilt top, using easing-in techniques as necessary.

ADDING A MITERED BORDER

1. With right sides together and raw edges aligned, center the top and bottom border strips along the top and bottom edges of the quilt center. (The border strips should overhang equally on each side of the quilt top.) Stitch the border strips to the quilt using a ¼"-wide seam, beginning and ending ¼" from the edge of the quilt center. Add the two side border strips, again centering them along the quilt edges, and beginning and ending the seam allowances ¼" from the edge of the pieced center. Your seams should meet in the corner, but not overlap. Press seam allowances out toward the edge of the quilt.

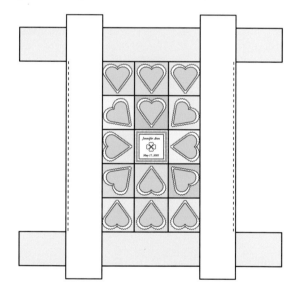

2. Fold the quilt diagonally, right sides together, aligning the top and side border seams to create a 45° angle. Confirm the angle by using a ruler with a 45° marking, and adjust as necessary.

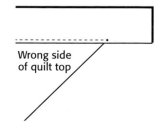

Wrong side of quilt top

3. Use the 45° marking on the ruler to mark the angle on the wrong side of the border strip.

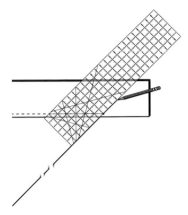

4. Stitch on the marked line. Open the corner prior to trimming, checking that the border strips meet neatly and that the corner will lie flat. Adjust if necessary.

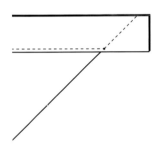

5. Trim ¼" from the marked line and press the mitered seam open.

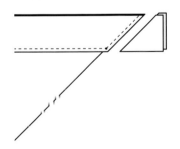

6. Repeat steps 2–5 on each remaining corner. Press the seam allowances out toward the quilt edge.

PREPARING THE BACKING

In general, backing fabric should be 3" to 5" larger than the quilt top on all four sides to allow ample yardage and uptake for quilting. The amount of extra backing can be reduced a bit for smaller projects, where less weight and stretch affect the quilting process. Adjust the yardage requirements and seaming as necessary if you are matching a directional print on the back.

A pieced backing is a great way to use up leftover yardage and blocks from the quilt. Stitch them together in any fashion to create all or part of the backing. Adjust the listed yardage accordingly.

Unless otherwise specified, use the following method and the yardage listed with the individual projects to make backing for any of the quilts in this book:

1. Cut the backing fabric in half, perpendicular to the selvage.

2. Place the two pieces right sides together.

3. Using a rotary cutter and ruler, trim the selvage edges.

4. Seam the two pieces together with a ¼" to ½" seam allowance.

5. Press the seams open.

LAYERING THE PROJECT

Most of the pieced tops we make are quilted by a professional long-arm quilter, which means that she does the layering. When we do layer a quilt, we typically tape the backing (right side down) to an uncarpeted floor or flat work surface, smooth the batting and pressed quilt top (right side up) over it, and use safety pins to secure the layers.

Spray basting works well for any project that can be quilted in one sitting, such as a quilted pillow top or table runner. Once again, choose your favorite method or product, or try something new to see if it makes sense to add to your own quilting repertoire.

QUILTING

There are many options for quilting, and each one will add something distinctive and special to your projects. A wonderful resource for quilting inspiration is *Quilting Makes the Quilt* (Martingale & Company, 1994) by Lee Cleland, who has supplemented a wealth of information on design, materials, marking, and methods with inspirational examples of the depth and vivacity that quilting provides to a project.

All of the larger quilts in this book were quilted by a professional long-arm quilter. If you choose this option, talk with other quilters or local quilt shops to get references. The quilting design, thread color, delivery date, and price range should always be clearly discussed, and even noted in writing when you give your project to a professional quilter.

Most of the small projects were quilted using a home sewing machine and a walking foot. Several of the projects are quilted using decorative stitches. No matter how you choose to quilt your project, always try out your design on a small scrap "quilt" as identical as possible to your finished piece. In doing so, you can troubleshoot the curves or corners in your quilting design, the stitch width or length, needle position, thread colors, machine tension, and more without the heartbreak of having to rip quilting out of an otherwise exciting project.

ADDING THE BINDING

Note: If you'd like to add a hanging sleeve to your quilt, do so prior to binding the edges. Refer to "Finishing Touches" on page 109 for instructions.

If you have not quilted all the way to the edge of the quilt top, use a walking foot to baste the quilted quilt less than ¼" from the edge with a widely spaced zigzag or straight stitch. This will reduce the possibility of the layers bunching up unevenly as you attach the binding. Choose the type of binding that's best for your project.

For quilts with straight edges, binding cut on the straight grain will work beautifully. For projects with curved edges, try bias binding. By cutting the strips at a 45° angle to the selvage, you will be able to create smoothly curved edges on your project.

For a traditional binding, cut strips 2½" wide. For a small project, such as a table runner, try using 2"-wide strips. The finished binding will be narrower and more in scale with the project.

❧ TIP ❧

A pieced binding will add one more playful element to a lighthearted quilt. Use the fabrics left over from the construction of the quilt top, cutting strips in lengths that vary from about 8" to 15" and joining them as described in the next section to provide the length needed to bind the quilt.

BASIC BINDING METHOD

1. With right sides together, join the binding strips by overlapping the ends at right angles as shown. Mark from one corner to the other, and stitch on the marked line.

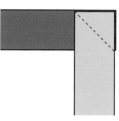

2. Trim the corners ¼" from the seam.

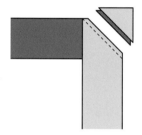

3. Press the seams open and trim the dog-ears to reduce bulk on the binding edge of your finished quilt.

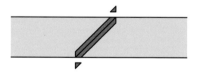

4. Trim the beginning end of the binding at a 45° angle; turn the angled edge under ¼" and press. Fold the strip in half lengthwise, wrong sides together, and press.

Fold line

5. Beginning several inches from a corner, and keeping the raw edges even, sew the binding to the front of the quilt using a ¼" seam allowance.

6. Stop sewing ¼" from the approaching corner and backstitch. Remove the quilt from the sewing machine.

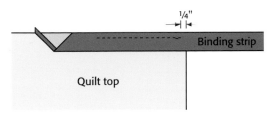

7. Fold the binding up to form a 45° angle, and then back down to align the raw edges of the quilt and the binding. Beginning at the edge, resume sewing the binding to the quilt. Repeat for the remaining corners.

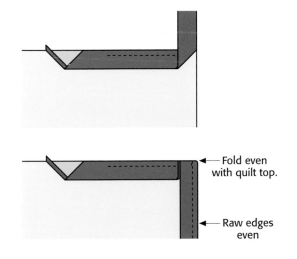

Fold even with quilt top.

Raw edges even

8. Fold the end piece of the binding into the starting end, overlapping by 2" to 3". Pin the overlap in place and complete the seam.

9. Turn the folded edge of the binding to the back of the quilt, forming miters at the corners. Whipstitch the binding into place, being sure to cover the seam.

Quilt back

FINISHING TOUCHES

Now all that's left is an optional step or two (or even three) to ensure that the quilt you've worked so hard to create will be appreciated, understood, and cherished, whether by the special people you know or a special stranger you've only met in your heart and imagination.

ADDING A HANGING SLEEVE

If you plan to display your quilt on a wall or in another venue, such as a quilt show, add a hanging sleeve to the back prior to adding the binding.

1. Cut a strip of fabric 10" wide, and 2" shorter than the width of the quilt top. Finish both 10" ends by making two ¼" turns along each edge toward the wrong side of the fabric; press and stitch.

2. Fold the strip in half lengthwise, right side out, and stitch ¼" from the raw edge. Press the seam open, and center it on the back of the tube; press.

3. Center the tube on the top edge of the back of the unbound quilt and baste, by hand or machine, the top edge of the tube onto the quilt ⅛" from the edge.

4. Stitch the binding into place as usual, as described on page 108 and at left. As you whipstitch the binding to the back of the quilt, you'll stitch through the tube to catch the quilt backing along the quilt's top edge. Finish the sleeve by whipstitching along the pressed bottom edge.

ADDING THE LABEL

A label adds a true finishing touch to a quilt, as well as the opportunity to give credit to the talented individuals involved in its creation. Use any medium that suits you: embroidery, permanent fabric-marking pens, appliqué techniques, or a combination of methods. Dress up the label by adding freehand or traced designs, a verse or poem, signatures, and—if you can bear to give your beautiful quilt away—the name of the lucky person receiving it!

The ideas in many of the sidebars throughout the book are easily adapted for making unique and highly personal labels. See "Picture Perfect: Working with Photos" on page 27, "Tips and Techniques for Decorative Stitching" on page 50, "Letter Perfect: Creating Distinctive Monograms" on page 54, and "All Tied Up! Working with Ribbon" on page 67.

At the very least, be sure to record names and dates, even if you only write them directly on the backing fabric with permanent fabric-marking pens. Finish by hemming the edges of your label and whipstitching it to the back of the quilt.

POCKET TREASURES

Oh, the allure of a pocket! The sweet anticipation of secrets to be shared or treasures to be discovered! A pocket allows the viewer to experience your project on multiple levels. It's more than beautiful, more than warm and cuddly…the contents of a pocket can conjure memories, calm fears on a dark night, or share your inspirations with everyone who enjoys your quilt.

What to place inside? Don't limit yourself to the ideas here…use your imagination!

- A charm on a ribbon string
- A favorite bedtime blessing or story written in your own hand
- A photograph of someone you love
- A history of the quilt to share with generations to come
- A sweet-smelling sachet
- A favorite poem or passage from a book
- A small flashlight or stuffed animal

TIP

Make multiple pockets, filling each with a memento or a portion of a story, as well as instructions on which pocket to open next!

---

1. Once you've decided what to tuck inside, decide how large the pocket should be, taking into account the bulk of the enclosed object and adding at least ½" to all sides. Cut a piece of fabric twice the size of the pocket. Fold opposite ends over ¼" to the wrong side of the fabric and press.

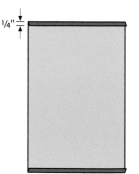

TIP

If the object you'll be placing in the pocket is bulky, cut the pocket larger than you think you'll need. Pin the pocket fabric in place, insert the object, and adjust the pocket size as necessary.

---

2. Fold the hemmed fabric in half right sides together as shown.

3. Stitch along the two raw edges. Clip the corners at the center fold, taking care not to cut into the seam.

4. Turn the pocket right side out; press. Finish the edges with a straight or decorative stitch.

5. Repeat steps 1–4 to make the pocket flap. Pin and hand stitch the pieces to the back of the quilted project. Add a button, snap, or hook-and-loop closure if desired.

BIBLIOGRAPHY

Cleland, Lee. *Quilting Makes the Quilt*. Woodinville, Washington: Martingale & Company, 1994.

Meredith Press. *Waverly at Home: Pillows*. Des Moines, Iowa: Meredith Books, 2001.

RESOURCES

Several of the projects in this book feature items we found in the inspiring and ever-changing selection of new and vintage ribbons and buttons at Button Emporium.

Button Emporium
914 SW 11th Ave.
Portland, OR 97205
503-228-6372
www.buttonemporium.com

Fabrics used with our inkjet printer to reproduce photographs shown in Pillow Talk on page 26 are by Click-n-Craft® from The Vintage Workshop®. Visit their site:

www.thevintageworkshop.com.

For a great online resource for monograms and downloads, visit:

www.embroideryarts.com

Fabrics for the Scotch Granny at the Beach Quilt and Scotch Granny at the Beach Throw shown on pages 90 and 93, respectively, are from Bali Fabrics. To view collections and find links to retailers, visit their site:

www.balifab.com

The stitching on several of the quilts and projects was done on Bernina machines. To view their full line of products and inspirations and find links to your local retailers, visit their site:

www.berninausa.com

ABOUT THE AUTHORS

Anne and Linda

Anne Moscicki and Linda Wyckoff-Hickey began Touchwood Quilt Design to create designs for quilters like themselves: busy women who place high value on their families and time, and enjoy creating projects that reflect personal style. Anne's childhood interests in art and crafts led her to combine a love of quilting with her award-winning career as an art director for print media. Linda picked up a needle and thread at age six, and never put them down as she began to design and sell unique clothing and custom-made quilts. Their combined talents have brought Touchwood Quilt Design into the homes and classrooms of tens of thousands of quilters. Anne lives with her husband, two daughters, and a spoiled-rotten West Highland terrier. Linda's home brims with the activities of her husband, four children, and a beautiful pair of faithful cats. Both Anne and Linda live in Lake Oswego, Oregon.